P9-CAL-431

Secrets of a
HAPPY
HEART

Other books by Hyveth Williams:

Anticipation
Will I Ever Learn?

To order, call 1-800-765-6955.

Visit us at **www.reviewandherald.com** for information on other Review and Herald® products.

★ ★ ★

Here's what they're saying about *Secrets of a Happy Heart:*

"This book presents a biblical worldview of what the Beatitudes and Christian life truly are, and it challenges the secular worldview that many Christians have unconsciously adopted. A must-read for anyone who truly wants to deepen their understanding of the abundant life God wants for us."

—*Rev. Denice Howard,* Pastor of Children's Ministries
First Baptist Church, Riverside, California

"*Secrets of a Happy Heart* is unlike any other book I've read on the Beatitudes—a total joy! Hyveth provokes the reader with a new perspective on a familiar Bible passage. The serious student of Scripture will treasure this work as a valuable resource for enhancing an understanding of this part of the much-loved Sermon on the Mount."

—*Rev. Mary Polite,* Pastor of Senior/Pastoral Care Ministries
First Baptist Church, Riverside, California

"An excellent book! Fascinating reading. Appropriate examples, good insights. An up-to-date look at a familiar but difficult passage. Pastor Williams challenges us to live out the Beatitudes boldly and wholeheartedly."

—*Rev. Diane Lutz,* Pastor of Adult Ministries
First Baptist Church, Riverside, California

"A fresh look at the Beatitudes that provokes us to reevaluate our intimate relationship with God, drawing the reader closer to the Lord."

—*Rev. Brenda J. Wood,* Pastor
New Life Christian Fellowship, Riverside, California

A Fresh Look at the Sermon on the Mount

HYVETH WILLIAMS

REVIEW AND HERALD® PUBLISHING ASSOCIATION
HAGERSTOWN, MD 21740

The author assumes full responsibility for the accuracy of all facts and quotations as cited in this book.

This book was
Edited by Gerald Wheeler
Copyedited by Delma Miller and James Cavil
Art direction and design by Ron J. Pride/square1studio
Interior design by Candy Harvey
Electronic makeup by Shirley M. Bolivar
Typeset: 11/14 Bembo

PRINTED IN U.S.A.

08 07 06 05 04 5 4 3 2 1

R&H Cataloging Service
Williams, Hyveth

Secrets of a happy heart: a fresh look at the Sermon on the Mount.
1. Sermon on the Mount. I. Title.

241.53

ISBN 0-8280-1810-3

Dedication

This book is dedicated to God and all His people who struggle to find the happy medium in a world beset by trials and tribulation.

Gratitude is also extended to my family and friends around the world,
especially
my son, Steven;
my grandson, Stephen;
my sister, Renita; and
Christy Robinson, Robin Baldwin, and Ella Taylor,
whose patience and enduring kindness helped to bring this idea to fruition.

I am especially grateful to the pastors in our women clergy group who took the time to review and comment on the manuscript.

Special appreciation goes to my Campus Hill church community, whose tender love and passion for the gospel have awakened me to seek and discover the secrets of a happy heart.

As we journey toward our goal of the second coming of Christ,
we will help each other open these cisterns of grace.

Contents

Foreword

A Happy Heart: It's a Way of Being

H'mm, aren't prefaces to spiritual books usually written by university scholars, professional clergy, and authorities on the book's subject? Did the author run out of those experts? Or did this pastor want an introduction by a member of the flock, the type of person who would be the book's consumer? Ah! Effective marketing strategist, this Pastor Hyveth!

That's what we call her at church, although we could call her Doctor Williams, Pastor Williams, or even Queen of the Hill. We tease her in e-mails, we lounge by her swimming pool on hot days, and we call her in racking sobs when we need comfort and advice. When she is vulnerable and emotionally bare, we weep with her. And when she (quite literally) jumps for joy, we can't help joining her. We never hesitate to say yes when she passes out jobs at the business meeting or work bee. As she supports a community project for unwed teen mothers or parents who have lost children to death, we are inspired to walk in Jesus' footsteps, touching the untouchable. When she began a class in New Testament Greek, just so we could study our Bibles with more depth, clarity, and vivid colors, we signed up and went the distance.

Hyveth says that with her, it's WYSIWYG. Wizzeewig? No, it's the acronym for What You See Is What You Get. She's not fake or phony. In fact, sometimes I (and presumably others) counsel her to be more cautious and less candid and outspoken. It's safer that way. But if there's such a sport as extreme pastoring, she's one of the hotshots. And she blazes the way in ministry for those of us who are not risk takers.

The great thing about our congregation is that we're encouraged to *be*, not *do*. The *doing* does happen, but the *being* is the foundation. That's probably the most profound lesson I've learned while in this fellowship of believers. It's the vast gulf between legalism and grace.

Our congregation is known for being culturally and racially diverse. A visitor whispered to me during a *Messiah* oratorio that she'd never seen so many cultures so graciously interacting as here. We don't have to act as if we tolerate each other. There's no toleration or acting to it. We just *are* parts of the body of Christ. They're parts of the whole, and we hardly notice any differences, except that they make up a gloriously colorful fabric of the Creator's design. Our pastor not only promotes that doing, but lives it, and we are *being* grace-filled.

I think that's exactly what God wants for us. *Being* and living up to His design. In Exodus 34 we read that Moses asked to see God, but the Lord said that to see His face would be death for Moses. So instead God described Himself to Moses in terms of character and *be-ing*. He said, I AM, I WILL BE WHO I WILL BE, compassionate, merciful, a "gracious God, slow to anger, abounding in love and faithfulness, maintaining love . . . forgiving" (Ex. 34:6, 7, NIV).

In 1 Corinthians 13 we see that love (and God is love) is patient, kind, not envious, not boastful, not proud, not rude or self-seeking, not easily angered; keeps no record of wrongs; rejoices in truth; is protective; always trusts and hopes and perseveres; and never fails. These are godly attributes.

Micah 6:8 says: "He has showed you, O man, what is good. And what does the Lord require of you? To act justly and to love mercy and to walk humbly with your God."

Do you see some cognate words in these passages? Compassion, mercy, love, humility, grace, slowness to anger, forgiving, loving. Those attributes of God are His greatest aspirations for us: to *be* like Him. Even the Ten Commandments are a description of who God is and what He does. He doesn't act or speak out of holy character (I through III), He rests after creating and working (IV), He honors the created by giving them rest and respect for human rights and a pleasant, peaceful lifestyle (IV through X). A godly person has those character traits written on the heart, not on stone blocks. All those descriptions of God are ways of *being* found in Christ, not ways of *doing* our salvation.

When Jesus sat on the Galilean hillside and spoke the Beatitudes, He told humans what would make them blissfully, deep-in-your-bones, everlastingly, richly happy—and that is to emulate Him, to have Him in their hearts. I believe that He had a smile on His face, and that He sometimes had to catch His breath from laughing. He wanted to communicate the joy that comes from an intimate fellowship with God. When Christ inhabits us body, mind, and soul, we have a sense of the fellowship of the Father, Son, and Spirit.

Jesus said to *be* joyful—dance! celebrate!—because His Beatitudes promise that we will be filled with the kingdom of God, be comforted, inherit the earth, be filled with righteousness, receive mercy, see God, be called sons of God, and be rewarded in heaven.

May you find joy as you read this book. I was blessed to hear the sermons as a sheep of Pastor Hyveth's flock, and to read them again as I edited the first draft of the manuscript. (You should see all the notes written in the margins of my Bible!) It is my desire that your Bible will become similarly marked as you read this book. The next time you're in a Bible study reading the Beatitudes, you'll be able to contribute some brilliant gem that will bless the class members, and let the light and beauty of our Savior shine more brightly.

What are you waiting for? Turn to chapter 1 right now!

—Christy K. Robinson
sheep of the flock, friend of the pastor
(also) public relations and marketing director
The Quiet Hour Echoes magazine editor
The Quiet Hour Worldwide Ministries
Redlands, California

CHAPTER

What Is Happiness?

"Down in the catacombs—those vast underground chambers of the dead where early Christians hid from their fierce persecutors—a stone bears this beautiful engravature: 'Felicissimus' (most happy)."—A. Naismith.

Looking pale and thin, Jenny sat across from me at the table. She was present with me in body, but seemed to be absent in mind as she pushed the food around her plate with a fork, toying with it like my cat disinterestedly bats toys or crumpled paper when its heart is not in the game. I tried to engage her in conversation so that she would raise her head and look at me.

Nervously trying to keep the conversation alive when I saw the tears slipping down her cheeks as her fingers shook uncontrollably, I reached across the table to place my hand on hers, to indicate that even though I truly did not know her inner struggle, I understood her pain. She pulled away with a quick jerking gesture, as if I had slapped her hand, before casting a fear-filled glance in my direction. The sadness in her eyes tore at my heart.

"Pastor," she started in a trembling voice. "Pastor," she repeated, breathing heavily after every word she struggled to speak, "I don't want to live anymore. I just want to die. I've been asking God to release me from this life, but each day I wake up and am forced to go through this ridiculous routine." She threw her fork onto the plate and shoved it from her, indicating that eating had become part of her "ridiculous routine."

Saying nothing, I simply leaned forward to convey to her that I was listening intently. I wanted to validate her pain and suffering, which was the result of a bitter second divorce from a second childless, unhappy relationship. The pain had really begun while she and her husband were dating. She had refused premarital counseling on the basis that her beloved fiancé believed that at age 40 (and a third marriage for him) they had both "figured out how to make things work."

Now she was embarrassed to look at me, knowing how hard and long I had pleaded with her not to put all her trust in their own experience, but to seek professional counseling. But I took no satisfaction in the fact that I had been right. None of God's children should hurt as deeply as Jenny did.

"Pastor," she said again, breaking into my reflections on how she could have avoided, or at least been equipped to handle, this situation had she listened to her heart and friendly, encouraging, supportive advice. "All I wanted was a family and a little happiness. Is that so terrible? How could God be so mean to me? I wasn't asking for that much, was I? All I was asking for was just a little bit of happiness." She held her thumb and index finger close together, almost touching, to demonstrate her meager desire for happiness. The grinch called misery had paid a lengthy visit to Jenny's life and refused to leave.

"I want to be happy! Not just for a moment, but for a lifetime." The movie star spoke defiantly as he glared at the audience of the popular talk show. The camera panned the room, showing close-ups of puzzled faces. The people seemed to be struggling to understand how one who had attained and possessed so much could be so miserable. After all, dressed in a most expensive Armani suit, he looked like a million dollars. Yet when the camera zoomed in, his bland stare and empty eyes peering out of black holes of pain confirmed the tale he was slowly admitting under the probing scrutiny of the talk-show host.

His story was a common struggle among many young, restless, rich, and famous people who had discovered that no amount of drugs or material possessions could fill the empty places of the heart. He had accomplished his dream of fame and fortune and had married some of the most beautiful women in the world. *People* magazine in its annual survey had touted him once as the sexiest man in the world and had listed him a close runner-up twice. But in the end the best he could say of his life was "I am the unhappiest man in the world."

In his quest for the illusive thing called happiness, he had risked everything on drugs and alcohol, for which he had gone to jail and endured humiliation, scrutiny, and vilification in the public media. He could not see the destructiveness of his behavior, because he was determined to experience all that the world promised would make him happy. In time he escaped into drugs to numb the agony of despair that wrenched his heart in his increasingly miserable existence.

Some two decades ago a popular song declared "Don't Worry, Be Happy!" It soared to the top of many musical charts around the world and continues to rank high among the most requested songs. Why? Because it touched a chord in the heart of everyone who heard it.

Happiness has been the desperate desire of every person born in this world since Adam and Eve found themselves cast out of the Garden of Eden. Advertisers and their commercial clients bank their future success on our insatiable quest for happiness by telling us that if we eat their cereals, drink their sodas, drive their cars, wear their designs, and listen to their CDs, we will all be deliriously happy. But we aren't! So what is this elusive thing called happiness?

Dear Abby once received a letter from a 15-year-old girl who defined happiness as having your own bedroom; having parents that are proud of you, trust you, forgive you, and don't fight; getting good grades in school; being well dressed and popular. She then told Abby that so far, happiness had passed her by.

Perhaps some of us share those sentiments, even if we know that they do not provide the answers we seek. At times feelings of hopelessness magnify our problems, coercing us into attempting to work things out our own way. Unfortunately, those ways do not really help. Nor can we escape our problems. Even in church we cannot avoid the real issues of life or the realization that the worshipers around us are often utterly indifferent to our pain. So where can we go to find a solution that will free us not just for a moment or a day but for a lifetime?

Shortly after she published the above letter, Dear Abby received a response from a 13-year-old, who wrote that happiness was being able to walk, talk, hear, and see. The writer had little sympathy for someone who could do all these and yet continue to be unhappy.

If we could find happiness in the abilities highlighted in the 13-year-old's letter, then the majority of the people in the world should be deliriously joyful. But time and experience have taught us that though physical, mental, and emotional health do make our lives a lot easier, they do not guarantee happiness. In fact, some of the world's most able-bodied men and women exist in a continuous state of misery. Others have sought happiness through blasphemous behavior reflecting their unbelief and rejection of divine truth and God. Still others have reluctantly admitted, often at the end of an empty, profligate life, that they never found the promised proverbial pot of gold at the end of the rainbow.

For example, Voltaire, one of the world's greatest infidels, proved that unbelief can never provide happiness. When he failed in his quest to find peace through every possible carnal desire in thought, word, or deed, the famous philosopher wrote and repeated publicly that happiness had eluded him. On his deathbed he wished that he had never been born.

Narcissism and pleasure seeking do not lead to happiness. Solomon, after decades of self-indulgence, admitted that he had failed to find true happiness. He said, "I have seen all the works which have been done under the sun, and behold, all is vanity and striving after wind" (Eccl. 1:14).

Centuries later the famous British aristocrat Lord Byron, whose life of pleasure seeking may have surpassed even that of Solomon, wrote at the end of his thoroughly dissolute life: "The worm, the canker, and grief are mine alone."

Wealth by itself does not bring happiness. A wise individual once cautioned: "Do not weary yourself to gain wealth, cease from your consideration of it. When you set your eyes on it, it is gone. For wealth certainly makes itself wings like an eagle that flies toward the heavens" (Prov. 23:4, 5).

In spite of the pressure and propaganda to get rich quick as part of the American, if not the universal, dream, money does not make men and women whole and happy. Ask many of the winners of million-dollar lottery jackpots. Years after the megabucks lotteries made those unsuspecting people millionaires, many have admitted in national news reports and magazine articles that the expected happiness also evaded them. Instead, greed destroyed some families, while long court battles related to the riches severed friendships and other relationships. Some winners found themselves penniless not long after accepting opportunities to sell the long-term annual endowments for short-term immediate cash bonanzas.

One man, in particular, who failed to meet his child-support commitment even though he had the financial resources, spent his entire fortune in a gambling casino. He ended up a pauper in jail, charged with fraud.

Jay Gould, a nineteenth-century American millionaire, who had plenty of money to waste and burn, left the world the following statement as a legacy: "I suppose I am the most miserable man on earth." He had learned the long, hard way that money cannot buy happiness.

Believers in Christ have come to know that true happiness does not consist in the possession of wealth or position, beauty or education, but in having a pure, clean heart cleansed by obedience to Him who is the truth and the life.

Happiness does not consist of a good posture or position. Today, almost every commercial in both visual and printed media would have us believe that if we can hold on to our youth and attain the right job, eat heartily, and maintain a supermodel's weight and measurements, we'll be extremely happy. To persuade us, they parade a bevy of nubile nymphets and full-fleeced jocks in a variety of seductive contortions on billboards and television. They have successfully convinced many of those fighting the vestiges of aging to buy their creams, follow their diets, drive their fast cars, and wear their ridiculous fashions. The epidemic of face-lifts, body tucks, weight-loss plans, and rooms filled with discarded exercise equipment proves that they've gotten through to us. Yet at the end of the day we are tired, fat, fearful, and miserable.

We should have listened to Lord Beaconsfield, another Briton who enjoyed more than his share of both youthfulness and position as a popular politician. A prestigious member of Parliament and descendant of peers, he declared, "Youth is a mistake; manhood a struggle; old age a regret."

It is only in true, undefiled religion, based on an intimate relationship with Christ, that we will discover the source of true happiness and health.

Nor is happiness found in military glory. Alexander the Great conquered the then-known world. Legend claims that when he realized that he had no more worlds to conquer, his soldiers heard him weeping uncontrollably in his tent late into the night, prior to passing out in a drunken stupor. His lament resulted from a deep, unquenchable thirst for fulfillment that had eluded him.

Before slipping into anonymity, many veterans of the Korean conflict, the Vietnam War, and Desert Storm have concluded that the momentary glory and adrenaline rush that accompanied the celebration of their wartime victory did not deliver the anticipated reward: happiness in retirement.

A former senator and presidential candidate shocked Americans when, during a presidential race, he revealed his secret of more than 30 years. Even though he had received the Purple Heart for his courageous actions in Vietnam and thereafter appeared to have adjusted well to the life of a popular, highly recognized, and admired war hero, he was miserable. For decades he had kept the secret that he had taken the lives of helpless women and children who, according to his testimony, had posed no threat to his safety or the security of his men. He told a news correspondent that not a day had passed since that event that he did not have images of that moment in his mind or bitterly regret his role in the incident.

He was haunted by the fear of discovery, convicted by his conscience about the evilness of that act, and crippled emotionally by the power of that devastating experience. When asked why he chose to reveal this secret after so many years, he responded that he had tried—and failed at all attempts—to regain joy in a life that lacked nothing materially. "The only way that I can experience happiness again is through the grace of God, which has given me the courage to take responsibility for my past actions and come clean to the American people who love and support me," he told a television reporter.

Yet even religion or religiosity cannot guarantee happiness. I am embarrassed to admit that some of the most miserable people I have met have been those practicing many types of religious beliefs. Those who have "a form of godliness" are not happy in Jesus, as they love to sing and shout, because their lives "have denied its power" (2 Tim. 3:5). The ones who have learned to be uptight with their long lists of do's and don'ts instead of being upright according to the Word and will of God seem to be the most miserable of all men and women.

Bill's experience is a powerful reminder of how religious fervor without the Holy Spirit can turn us into mean-spirited Pharisees who rob others of their happiness in Christ. He was once a successful professor and pianist living out the American dream with his family in the suburbs. The devastating death of his only child turned his life into a nightmare. His peaceful existence spiraled quickly out of control into the loss of everything he treasured, until he ended up homeless, living on the streets of his city. For several years he struggled to survive in that concrete jungle by sleeping under bridges.

One rainy day another homeless man discovered a book in the garbage through which he had been rifling for food. Unfortunately, it was soaking wet and all the pages were stuck together. He took it to the place where Bill was sitting, placed it on a rock in the sun where it would dry, and left to continue scavenging for food and clothing in the garbage dump nearby.

An educated man, Bill had once loved to read, but had forgotten the pleasure of a good book. Although he had avoided the trap of cheap alcohol, he would have been glad for a sip from any brown bag that day as his stomach growled and he shivered under the cold, wet rags draped around his emaciated body. As he sought a warm spot in the sun he saw the other homeless man place the book on the rock. As he watched the pages of the book, he noticed that as they dried the wind blew them free and flipped them over, leaving the book open. The sight intrigued him, especially in his world of long days and nights with nothing but loneliness and emptiness to mark time. So he drew closer to watch as page after page dried and flopped over.

As he leaned forward he suddenly realized the book was a Bible. The pages kept turning in the breeze, then stopped. Then his eyes landed on one verse: "Then I will make up to you for the years that the swarming locust has eaten" (Joel 2:25). Without giving a thought to how ridiculous his actions might have seemed, he looked up into the sky, thumped his chest, and cried out, "God, I'm a really good candidate to prove Your stuff! If You are really God, restore me and my losses!"

No bushes burst into flame, nor did angels appear, harp in hand, to serenade or whisk him away to food and family. Instead, he took the Bible, which was now dry, and went to a shelter where he was always able to get a hot meal.

Several years before, in the very beginning of his homelessness, when he still had hopes of being rescued by at least the welfare system that he had supported while gainfully employed, Bill had applied for assistance but was denied it. He had given the address and telephone number of this particular shelter that he had frequented back then. But when the authorities repeatedly turned down his applications, he had given up and gone deeply into the homeless subculture that thrives in almost every city.

Time had fully erased the memories of those days, so when the proprietor came to tell Bill that he had a telephone call, it stunned him. To his surprise, he learned that his 5-year-old application for assistance had been finally approved and that his first check was on the way.

Within days Bill had the check in his hands. Still clinging to the Bible that the other homeless man had left behind and forgotten, he was able to secure a room, take a long-awaited bath, and begin the journey back to wholeness as a beloved son of God. One of the first things he did with that first check was to purchase a small black-and-white television at a yard sale he happened on while strolling through his new neighborhood. As he flipped channels to find a worship service he used to watch before he became homeless, he saw a program with one of my videotaped sermons and was profoundly moved by it. The experience made such an indelible impression on his mind that he summoned up the courage to visit my office during the following week.

Soon Bill began Bible studies. He attended church, never missing even the midweek services. We all watched the transformation, both physically and spiritually, but one thing never changed. Bill treasured his beautiful long white hair and beard, which made him look like a slimmed-down version of Santa Claus.

On the day he joined our church he wore a dark-blue suit that a friend had kept for him in the hope that one day he would return from the streets to wear it. He told how he had not cut his hair and beard in years, but on that special occasion had visited a barber to have them trimmed so that he could present himself properly to God and His people. At Bill's request the barber cut his hair close to what he thought the hair of Jesus looked like—long, straight, flowing onto his shoulders—but left the beard untouched. Bill also said that he had been so excited that the barber thought he was getting married. When Bill explained that he was joining a church, the barber tried to discourage Bill, because "Christians are such hypocrites." He used every ploy he knew to prevent Bill from making "such a disastrous decision." But Bill was too happy to be dissuaded. He surprised the barber by insisting that a group with the shortcomings he underscored was exactly the kind of people who would accept a recovering homeless person as a member, ones with whom he would personally feel most comfortable.

Two weeks after Bill joined our church, a visitor who paraded his conservative, fundamental religious heritage like a badge of honor attacked Bill for his beard and hair. He was determined to "straighten" out Bill. The man was a modern-day Pharisee, because at one point he declared that it was a sin for anyone to accept a bribe. Yet shortly after expounding on the subject and realizing that he had not been able to convince Bill to get his hair and beard cut, he tried to coerce him into accepting a bribe to go to the barber. When Bill graciously rejected his offer, he became incensed, belligerent, even obnoxious, as he demanded that Bill concede to his request or face being shunned by him and other legalistic members.

"You are a disgrace to God with your hair and beard looking like Santa Claus," he scolded Bill in a futile attempt to manipulate him by undercutting his self-esteem.

"But Pastor Williams has never mentioned this to me during our Bible studies," Bill retorted.

"She was obviously too embarrassed to say anything to you," the present-day Pharisee replied arrogantly. Without taking the time to get to know Bill, to hear his story, to discover the tremendous journey through which God had brought him thus far and the reason Bill wanted to keep his beautiful hair and beard, the visitor insisted, "She did not want to tell you how awful you look. You will never be able to get a job or be accepted in our church."

That sort of legalism always disgusts me. I didn't have the energy even to imagine the effort it would take to repair the emotional damage that I feared might be more than enough to propel Bill into despair and send him fleeing from our fellowship. But I decided to wait a few days before contacting him, more to give me a chance to recover my own peace of mind than to avoid the outrage I expected to hear from Bill.

To my surprise, when I spoke to him a few days later, he was as warm and charming as he had always been. "I'm sorry for what that man said to you." I spoke quickly before Bill could speak. "He is not one of our members—he was a visitor and a stranger," I added, desperately trying to apologize for the incident.

"Pastor," Bill said reassuringly, "I must admit that I had the wind kicked out of me for a moment when he attacked me. But later, as I reflected on the fact that this man had moments before declared it a sin to take a bribe, yet was pressing me to accept one from him when no one was noticing, I realized that his was not the right spirit. He was not able to steal my joy," Bill assured me. Sometimes it is out of the mouths of born-again babes that some of the most profound spiritual truths come from God to us.

He had quickly discovered that happiness was in the "being" in Christ and not in the "doing" demands of legalism. So where is happiness found, if not in strict adherence to religious codes and patterns of behavior, personal worth, possessions, talents, reputation, accomplishments, applause, and kudos from others? Is it in the blizzard of spiritual self-help books proposing formulas for prayer, peace, and power? Absolutely not! It is found in one Person alone—Jesus Christ, the Creator of heaven, earth, people, plants, and animals.

Jesus clearly defined what constitutes true happiness in the inspired reports of the four Gospels. He also demonstrated in His life on earth that we will find true happiness, not in the indulgence of pride and luxury, but in devoted communion with God through His created works and written Word. The condition of eternal happiness lies only in perpetual obedience to the Word and will of God. He left us a rich legacy of happiness that is neither the creation of secular societies nor the product of sinfully delicious ideas, but a divinely ordained experience to be treasured by all God's children.

When I first became a believer, many of my secular friends moaned that I would never enjoy normal life again. They had the idea that Christianity was a giant black hole, a dismal cave of misery devoid of "happy hours" and nightspots where the music never stops, for those were our definitions of happiness. But thank God that very early in my Christian walk I read a statement that set me on a course to experience, embrace, and enjoy the fullness of life God has prepared for us.

The writer said: *"The religion of Christ does not obliterate or even weaken a single faculty. It in no way incapacitates you for the enjoyment of any real happiness;* it is not designed to lessen your interest in life, or to make you indifferent to the claims of friends and society. It does not mantle the life in sackcloth; it is not expressed in deep-drawn sighs and groans. No, no; *those who in everything make God first and last and best are the happiest people in the world"* (*Messages to Young People,* p. 38; italics supplied).

The words of one of my favorite children's songs seem to sum up the matter:

"Happiness is to know the Savior,
Living a life within His favor,
Having a change in my behavior—
Happiness is the Lord.
Happiness is to be forgiven,
Living a life that's worth the livin',
Taking a trip that leads to heaven—
Happiness is the Lord.
Real joy is mine, no matter if the teardrops start;
I've found the secret, it's Jesus in my heart."

For those who, like me, are desperately in need of and searching for consistent happiness that will last a lifetime and beyond, please note that Jesus took and takes human happiness very seriously. In fact, it was so important to Him that of all the words He used repeatedly, "happiness" ranks at the top of the list. He made it clear to the disciples He chose and trained, as well as the multitudes that listened in as He prepared them for ministry, that at the heart of the kingdom of God is His plan for our happiness. To demonstrate this, He used the word "happy" nine times in the Sermon on the Mount, also popularly referred to as the Beatitudes (Matt. 5:3-12). He also mentioned them four times in the Sermon on the Plain (Luke 6:20-22). In these beatitudes Jesus gave nine character traits that we are about to explore. They are the gateway to authentic inner happiness and the identification of a true believer.

The word for "happiness" also appears prominently in seven "beatitudes" in the last book of the Bible (Rev. 1:3; 14:13; 16:15; 19:9; 20:6: 22:7, 14). The apostle Paul uses it three times in his letter to the Romans (Rom. 4:7, 8; 14:22), and it appears once in the fourth Gospel (John 20:29).

In all of these cases translators, and some authors of paraphrases of the New Testament, used the word "blessed," from the Latin *beatitudo.* The early Church Fathers chose *beatitudo* when they translated the Bible from Greek to Latin. Those early translators wanted to convey a "state of utmost bliss," the meaning of their word and the original connotation of the Greek word. However, it got transposed to the word "blessed" that is used almost thoughtlessly, as a cliché, especially after a sneeze.

The word "blessed" is a good, powerful word, even though it was not the one Jesus and the other inspired writers of the Bible used to convey the concept of happiness. "Blessed" comes from the Greek word *eulogeo,* which means, literally, "to speak well of; to praise, to celebrate with praises addressed to God, acknowledging His goodness, with desire for His glory."

Jesus "eulogized" or spoke well of the food (Matt. 14:19) before breaking the five loaves and two fishes to feed 5,000 men and an unknown number of women and children as well as when He instituted the Lord's Supper (Matt. 26:26). He also said that His followers are to "bless [speak well of] those who curse you, [and] pray for those who mistreat you" (Luke 6:28).

When Jesus gave the Sermon on the Mount, He specifically and deliberately chose the word *makarioi,* which originally meant "rich," but was later employed to convey "happy" sentiments. He opted for this term to describe and extol the eternal riches of inner happiness that come from the godly blessings enjoyed by believers.

Homer, who wrote the *Iliad* and the *Odyssey* during the 800s B.C., also used *makarioi* to describe abundant, outward prosperity.

We should not confuse the word with our English meaning of happiness. In English it denotes good fortune, prosperity, a state of well-being, contentment, and pleasurable or satisfying experiences, all of which are indeed part of *makarioi,* but not the full extent of it.

I am underscoring this explanation because we generally associate our word "happiness" with the brief, instantaneous subjective state that is the result of happenstance, an event, circumstance, or chance occurrence. On the other hand, *makarioi* has its genesis in a word that means "large, long, and lengthy," which Jesus chose to use because He intended to pronounce not only temporary inner bliss, but also passions and emotional experiences that once attained in Him would last forever.

Behind the New Testament use of the word "happy" lies the understanding that it is the opposite of sin. Sin is the fountainhead of all misery, mental illness, disease, and social, political, and spiritual deprivation. When Jesus employed *makarioi*—"happy"—to introduce the principles of His newly inaugurated, invisible kingdom on earth, He offered it as holiness, the final frontier and effectual cure for every human hurt and woe caused by sin. He placed this word in the rich environment of virtues such as faith, hope, joy, and love.

This concept left an indelible impression on the mind of John, the beloved disciple. So much so that when he introduced his letter to the seven churches he declared, "Happy is he who is reading, and those hearing, the words of the prophecy, and keeping the things written in it—for the time is nigh" (Rev. 1:3, YLT). When he was given the revelation of the doom of those who worshipped the beast (Rev. 14:9-12), he also noted that the heavenly messenger who opened these truths to him thundered loudly, saying: "Happy are the dead who in the Lord are drying from this time" (verse 13, YLT).

Happiness was the keynote of Jesus' preaching. Not once, but nine times, Jesus repeated the word "happy," seeking to press this great idea deep into the minds of His disciples. He wanted them to know and understand that although they had sacrificed everything—lucrative professions, political goals, or family and friends—to follow Him, they were going to be happy in the end. Jesus could confidently promise that they would inherit happiness because the gospel is good news of great happiness.

Even though the word *makarios* appears frequently in the New Testament, it is almost always used in direct beatitudes addressed to people. Only occasionally does it involve other things such as eyes and ears (Matt. 13:16) and the womb (Luke 11:27). In addition to the Beatitudes, the book of Matthew has Jesus using the term again and again in ways that have no parallel in the other Gospels.

He said to His disciples, Happy is the one "who does not take offense in Me" (Matt. 11:6). Jesus told them, "Happy are your eyes because they see, and your ears because they hear" (Matt. 13:16, YLT). And after He pressed the disciples for answers to His question "Who do you say I am?" Simon Peter answered: "You are the Christ, the Son of the living God" (Matt. 16:15, 16, NIV). Christ then declared: "Happy art thou, Simon Bar-Jona, because flesh and blood [human heart, mind, and understanding] did not reveal [it] to thee, but my Father who is in the heavens" (verse 17, YLT).

At the close of His earthly ministry Jesus warned His disciples then and now to live every day in a state of alertness and readiness for His second coming. He also added, to the joy of believers: "Happy that servant, whom his lord, having come, shall find doing so" (Matt. 24:46, YLT).

The reality, however, is that we live in a world where time seems to be winding down to the last day of the great judgment. And our society offers little or nothing that approaches the virtues expressed in these beatitudes and the beginning of the Sermon on the Mount. Pride in self overcomes poverty of spirit. Pleasure seekers outnumber mourners. Instead of meekness we struggle with arrogance and "attitude." No longer hungering after righteousness, many seem to be declaring, "I am rich, and have become wealthy, and have need of nothing" (Rev. 3:17). Cruelty and violence have swept away mercy. Immorality floods our world. We drink it in from the moment of conception, and as soon as we are able to recognize images we are served generous portions from the entertainment industry. Lawsuits for the slightest reason threaten the peacemakers, and resentment and quarrels are no longer merely marked by harsh words, but instead settled with knives and guns. Rather than rejoicing in and through mistreatment, we fight back with every available weapon.

At times feelings of hopelessness overwhelm us. Problems seem so great in contrast to our puny attempts to resolve them. At other times the struggle with what Chuck Swindoll described as "those demoralizing seasons of dark depression" that "include discouraging feelings that refuse to go away" seems to suck us into an abyss of despair. When we find ourselves in those moods we must read the Beatitudes again and again until we finally grasp their significance for the circumstances and situations of our lives. Then we will discover, as we are about to in this book, that they are truly the blueprint for happiness and the answer to the perpetual questions about our purpose in life.

The teaching of Jesus in the Beatitudes is a guide to human happiness born out of intimate contact with real human needs. In touch with our deep, secret thoughts and feelings, it provides the only effective remedy for hopelessness and despair. We can exercise no greater wisdom than to listen and adhere to the words He later supported with deeds mightier than any other human has ever performed on earth.

If you are in a spiritual rut, read on. Or if you are the hapless victim of the seven deadliest "misses"—misguided, misinformed, misused, mistrust, mishandled, misunderstood, and mistaken—this book is definitely for you.

On the other hand, if you feel that you've got it made and that you are the center of your universe, if you are confident that there is absolutely no sorrow you cannot heal or handle, don't put this book down. There's also something surprising and special in it for you.

Discover with me that the Beatitudes are not a set of rules and regulations, but a set of profound principles about the life we are to, and will, live when the Holy Spirit is getting His way with us. This book will free you from the burdens of pride, presumption, and pretense.

And above everything else, it will make you very happy!

CHAPTER

The Paradox of Poverty

"Happy the poor in spirit—because theirs is the reign of the heavens."
Matthew 5:3, YLT.

Late one evening a man steered a large tanker full of highly flammable chemicals through a mountainous region. Being unfamiliar with such terrain, he drove cautiously as he carefully maneuvered his cargo through the winding roads that became steeper with each passing mile and darkening moment. After almost an hour he began feeling more comfortable with his handling of the now-monotonous turns as he climbed higher and higher.

He had barely relaxed from the tension caused by the narrow road when he encountered an unexpectedly steep downward grade. The tanker quickly picked up speed. Panicking, he slammed his foot on the brakes, twisting his body across the steering wheel as he turned it sharply, with every ounce of his strength, to bring the vehicle back under control. The sudden braking caused the tank to jackknife, hurling the trailer down the steep precipice and dragging the cab along with it. The violent maneuver threw the driver from the cab onto the craggy precipice. He grabbed a withered limb of a dead tree and held on for dear life. The tank plunged to the bottom of the ravine and burst into flames, sending a black mushroom cloud into the air below him.

The driver, in a predicament, looked around. Thinking he could swing himself onto a ledge and climb to safety on the large rock looming above him, he discovered that his legs were badly bruised and broken. As he weighed his options, he noticed that the small pebbles supporting the huge rock above him were now beginning to slide swiftly down the side of the precipice. His fear increased even more when the rock, dislodged by the force of the tank's plunging impact, began to loom precariously above him, threatening to crush him to death. The snapping sounds of the tree branch to which he clung made him realize that his only chance of survival was quickly slipping away.

Summoning all his strength, the man shouted at the top of his lungs, "He . . . lp! Is anyone up there?" He had hoped a passing motorist would have noticed the damaged barriers along the edge of the road or the flames shooting up out of the ravine. To his great relief, a calm voice broke the silence, saying, "This is God. I am here to help you. Do exactly as I say."

"I will! I will!" the driver replied passionately without waiting for the instructions. The voice continued calmly, carefully instructing the driver to "let go of the limb." He quickly assessed his situation. The rock above the ledge had shifted and was about to crash down on him. His weight had pulled the tree to which he clung partially out of the ground, dislocating pebbles and particles of dirt that pelted him in the face.

The driver looked below him and realized that should he let go of the limb, he would plunge to sudden death in a blazing inferno of poisonous chemicals. So he made a quick decision. Breathing in deeply to fill his lungs, already aching from the chemicals that poisoned the air around him, the man screamed with all his might, "Is there anyone else up there?"

If you are afraid of attempting the impossible, avoid the first beatitude. Don't come near it! It challenges us to let go of every vestige of what we consider security. In a world in which the motto seems to be "the one who dies with the most toys wins," this beatitude says that the poor in spirit are happy. That "the way to a deeper knowledge of God is through the lonely valleys of soul poverty and abnegation of all things. The blessed ones who possess the kingdom are they who have repudiated every external thing and have rooted from their hearts all sense of possessing" the "my" and "mine" spirit of the age (A. W. Tozer, *The Pursuit of God,* p. 23).

This beatitude suggests that deliverance from the human lust to be powerful will happen only when we are powerless and no longer in control of our destiny. It also admonishes us to trust that the Lord does hear the poor (Ps. 69:33) and has compassion on the needy and will save them

(Ps. 72:13). The first beatitude calls us to have the same attitude that Christ Jesus had (Phil. 2:6-8) when He gave up everything. Whatever we treasure, we must release and relinquish it all, surrender and submit to the Father, as Jesus did. Only then will we be happy. It makes us realize that the governing principles of the kingdom of God are always opposite and contrary to the world's rules. For, just as the old saying suggests that "cleanliness is next to godliness," this beatitude informs us that lowliness is the beginning of holiness.

Our fallen human nature covets things with a fierce and deep passion. As a result, the first beatitude is a hard saying to our generation, which seeks to avoid poverty at any cost. The modern drive to be rich and successful marginalizes those who are poor (in any aspect of the human experience).

Several years ago I produced 12 audiotape lessons on the Beatitudes entitled *Bold, Beautiful, Blessed*. At that time I focused on the significance of spiritual poverty during the time of Jesus. In His day only the rich could devote their time to studying the Torah to learn how to become ritually pure. The poor had to do manual labor and thus had no education or time to study the Torah, being too busy just surviving to be able to seek God's favor. It left them permanently ritually impure. The people of Israel, a majority of whom were peasants painfully eking out a meager existence under the harsh hands of a religious ruling class, were taught that poverty was a sign of God's disfavor. Thus when Jesus unveiled the principles of His kingdom in the Sermon on the Mount, He began by affirming that "happy [are] the poor in spirit" (YLT), for "theirs is the kingdom of heaven" (NKJV).

His teaching was a dramatic departure from—and marked contrast to—the teachings of the scribes and Pharisees who had taken their usual places in front of the crowd to challenge and entrap Jesus so they could destroy His increasing popularity with the masses. As the educated guardians of the Word and will of God, they demonstrated their spiritual power and divine favor by such things as the size of their phylacteries. These were two small square leather boxes containing the Ten Commandments and other scriptural passages worn on the left arm and forehead (see Matt. 23:5).

I am certainly not among those who promote the idea that Jesus was saying poverty guarantees spirituality. While there is no virtue or disgrace in being poor, neither does it, in itself, produce humility or purity in heart. Anyone who has ever visited an urban ghetto or a poverty-stricken rural village knows that. The indigent can struggle with pride just as much as the wealthy.

I believe, however, that poverty of spirit—a spiritual grace—is a fruit that grows only on a tree nurtured by the Holy Spirit and pruned by the loving hand of God. Sadly, the great majority of those who claim to be called by Christ's name lack real poverty of spirit. A. W. Tozer said that "egotism, exhibitionism, self-promotion [and a host of other self-sins]—are strangely tolerated in Christian leaders, even in circles of impeccable orthodoxy" (*The Pursuit of God,* p. 43).

Many leaders feed on pride instead of starving the lusts of the flesh. They fail to teach others how to search their hearts and submit to God (Ps. 139:23, 24).

At the time I did the audiotapes I suggested that to be poor in spirit is to realize that one has nothing, is nothing, and can do nothing without God's empowering presence in one's life. It certainly does not mean that one is nothing more than a worm, as some conjecture based on a verse in Psalm 22. Rather, poverty of spirit is a consciousness of one's emptiness without God. It means a complete absence of pride in the mind, personality, or passion. The spiritually poor have discovered that all my own righteousness is as filthy rags (Isa. 64:6) and realize that even our best attempts to win a place in the kingdom of grace are unacceptable. Such "self-help" works are an abomination to our holy God, who sent His only begotten Son to offer us the true, *free gift* of eternal life.

Those who are poor in spirit realize that they are nothing in their own sight, even if an admiring world does regard them as special. The regenerated, reconsecrated, born-again person is willing to say with David, "Since I am afflicted and needy, let the Lord be mindful of me. You are my help and my deliverer; do not delay, O my God" (Ps. 40:17). To them belong the kingdom of heaven.

On my tapes I also appealed to all who seek to be sons and daughters of God not to delay, but to act immediately to include themselves among those bequeathed God's kingdom. One day, more than a year later, as I was reading Matthew 5:1-12 again, I noticed that Jesus' number one priority in the newly inaugurated kingdom of God dealt with the malady that all of us suffer—the desire for power in our quest to find happiness.

Let us therefore examine the concept of being poor in spirit, so we can discover how we can apply this first principle, which announces: "Happy [are] the poor in spirit," for "theirs is the kingdom of heaven."

Jesus delivered the Sermon on the Mount shortly after He officially began His ministry. Up until that time He had lived in Nazareth in Galilee, traveling as an itinerant teacher and preacher around the region of His hometown. He had only a few disciples, and they continued to pursue their traditional livelihood, following Him only intermittently during that first year of His ministry.

The time came, however, when Jesus had to move away from Nazareth (Matt. 4:12, 13). After His first sermon in the local synagogue, based on Isaiah 61:1, 2 (see Luke 4:14-21), in which He set forth His mission, the people began "speaking well of Him, and wondering at the gracious words which were falling from His lips" (verse 22). The popular reaction filled the religious leaders with jealousy and rage, especially when He zoomed in on their specific shortcomings (verses 23-27). So they "got up and drove Him out of the city, and led Him to the brow of the hill on which the city had been built, in order to throw Him down the cliff" (verse 29).

Jesus then moved to Capernaum, where the citizens accepted His ministry with awe and admiration. His popularity also increased tremendously, as people "were amazed at His teaching, for His message was with authority" (verse 32).

Capernaum was a great place for His headquarters. It was a regional commercial center, located on one of the main trade routes to Damascus to the northeast, the Mediterranean cities of Tyre and Sidon to the northwest, and Jerusalem to the southwest. The village of perhaps 1,500 people was an important toll station on the border of the territories of Herod Antipas and Herod Philip. As a result, it was an ideal location from which His teaching and preaching could spread to all parts of Galilee and even the world beyond.

Peter, one of the first disciples who had been following Jesus sporadically for almost a year, also lived in Capernaum. Whenever Jesus was in town, Peter opened his home to Him (Matt. 8:14). From there they often launched out on short mission trips to teach and preach, and to heal the people who came to hear them.

After relocating His headquarters in Capernaum sometime during the summer of A.D. 29, Jesus made an extended evangelistic tour of the cities, towns, and villages of Galilee. To get an idea of how major a journey it was, we refer to Josephus, the Jewish historian. Josephus said that "Galilee was a densely populated region dotted by over 200 towns and villages."

The description of His tour in the four Gospels suggests that Jesus may have visited all of those towns and villages. He taught with divine authority and healed those struggling with all kinds of diseases. Reports of what He did (or rumors, as the Greek word describes it) spread instantly throughout the region. The result was inevitable. Great multitudes came from all parts of Palestine and the Decapolis to hear and be healed.

No political rally or stadiums filled with thousands of screaming sports or music fans could have surpassed the outpouring of people as Jesus' ministry flourished. It was during this period that He appointed a permanent group of disciples, beginning with the first four who had followed him intermittently. He challenged them to leave their full-time occupation of netting live fish, destined to die, to catch dead men ordained to live by God's grace. Later Jesus also called another eight from the more than 70 who accompanied Him around the region (see Luke 10:1) after the majority of them withdrew when they heard some of the "hard sayings" Jesus presented to the Jews in the synagogue at Capernaum (see John 6:41-70).

After ordaining the twelve (Luke 6:12-16), Jesus took His disciples away from their families to His seminary in nature to train them for ministry. Then He "gave them power and authority over all the demons and to heal diseases. And He sent them out to proclaim the kingdom of God and to perform healing" (Luke 9:1, 2).

I am really glad the record shows that Jesus trained them before sending them out. It should silence the protests of those who think that when Jesus calls and anoints people for ministry, they do not need any further education.

While He was walking along the lakeshore teaching His disciples, multitudes kept pouring onto the shoreline. Some hobbled along on crude crutches fashioned from tree limbs. Others, too weak to walk, had family and friends carry them on rough mats and hastily constructed litters. Some waded into the water, screaming and reaching out to touch Him, like crazed fans at a rock concert.

Soon the mob pushed the disciples out of their way so that they could get close enough to touch or be touched by Jesus. "When Jesus saw the crowds, He went up on the mountain; and after He sat down, His disciples came to Him. He opened His mouth and began to teach them" (Matt. 5:1, 2).

Jesus had prepared Himself for this great demand on His time and attention. In his account of this historic event and notable day, Luke tells us that "it was at this time that He [Jesus] went off to the mountain to pray, and He spent the whole night in prayer to God" (Luke 6:12). Even Jesus, the God-man, spent the night in prayer before He approached significant events in His life! What then should we mere mortals do?

Sometimes it surprises me that I myself, who preach and teach the gospel, will so easily become tyrannized by time and pressed by the immediate that I will rush into making important decisions without taking the appropriate time to pray. We must put an end to such foolhardy behavior and take time to pray before we do anything.

No one knows which Galilean mountain became His seminary that day, even though Christian scholars refer to it as the "Sinai of the New Testament." Some also posit that the Sermon on the Mount, in which Jesus gave the manifesto of the kingdom of God, is to Christianity what Mount Sinai is to Judaism, where God proclaimed the Ten Commandments, the divine law, and covenant to Moses and ancient Israel.

On that unknown hillside in Galilee Jesus reaffirmed the divine law, explaining its true meaning in greater detail and in practical ways. He applied its precepts to the problems of daily living so that the uneducated fishermen and poor peasants could learn and understand. That morning after His night of prayer, "Jesus came down with them and stood on a level place, and there was a large crowd of His disciples, and a great throng of people from all Judea and Jerusalem, and the coastal region of Tyre and Sidon, who had come to hear Him and to be healed of their diseases; and those who were troubled with unclean spirits were being cured. And all the people were trying to touch Him, for power was coming from Him and healing them all" (verses 17-19).

Seated on the grass were also spies, sent by the Sadducees and Pharisees. They had instructions to report anything the religious leaders might be able to use against Him to destroy His growing popularity and influence.

Anxious fathers clutched the hands of sick children as they pushed their way forward in the crowd. Mothers clasped their infants to their bosom. The blind stumbled, and the crippled hobbled painfully up the side of that mountain. All needed help that only Jesus could provide.

What do you think their emotions and expectations were? If you were in their situation, what would your emotions and expectations be? What are they now, as you consider your own personal search for satisfaction, peace, joy, and that elusive thing called happiness? Imagine yourself right there, in the center of this scene, listening to Jesus with great anticipation.

The disciples, it appeared, believed that the kingdom would soon be established. The events of the morning convinced them that Jesus was about to announce its inauguration. Their feeling of expectancy also pervaded the people, whose eager faces revealed their deep interest in what was about to happen. As the multitude sat upon the green hillside, awaiting the words of Jesus, hope must have filled their hearts. Political zealots longed for Jesus to employ His mighty power to free Palestine from the despised Roman occupiers. Some of the scribes and Pharisees, although they hated Jesus, were still willing to use His tremendous gifts to overcome Rome. The poor peasants and fishermen, on the other hand, just wanted assurance that their lives might someday consist of more than wretched hovels, scanty food, and unending toil.

The currents of excitement that rippled through the crowds indicated that their hearts thrilled with the hope that Israel would once again be honored before the nations as the chosen of the Lord, and that Jerusalem would be exalted as the head of God's universal kingdom. But Jesus disappointed all their hopes of worldly gain when He declared, "Happy [are] the poor in spirit." For, instead of giving them a fish to satisfy their immediate hunger, He taught them how to go fishing for happiness in the eternal pond called grace.

The word "poor" also means "beggar," i.e., one who cowers and crouches in fear like the common beggars in Jerusalem. "Spirit," on the other hand, in this verse does not refer to God, the Holy Spirit, nor the temper or disposition of mind or outlook, but "breath," the essential element and vital principle that gives life. Jesus was therefore speaking of the poverty in spirit that results from possessing nothing—or from not being possessed by anything.

All the descendants of Adam and Eve have crouched and cowered in fear in the presence of God ever since the first couple ate the fruit against His instructions (Gen. 2:17). The reality is that ever since that day we have been naked and ashamed, miserable beggars in a world overwhelmed by satanic powers.

The problem, however, is that we have fashioned fig leaves in a variety of mental, emotional, and even physical garments to cover our unhappy condition of alienation from God. At the same time, we struggle to hide the emotional isolation that strains all our relationships while we busily attempt to convince ourselves that we are "rich, and have become wealthy, and have need of nothing" (Rev. 3:17). The truth is that regardless of what we look like on the outside, without God we are "wretched and miserable and poor and blind and naked" on the inside (verse 17).

When Jesus addressed the "poor in spirit" He was also alluding to the common nickname, "poor breather," that the affluent landowners and religious rulers in His day gave to the peasants. Wealthy rulers not only oppressed those of low social status with heavy burdens of taxes and religious requirements, but also taunted them for having nothing but the breath they breathed. They considered poverty a sign of divine disfavor. The lives of the poor became even more miserable because of the teaching that God would not save landless laborers.

William Barclay, in his classic commentary *The Gospel of Matthew,* expanded on the meaning of "poor in spirit." He said that "these words in Hebrew underwent a four-stage development of meaning. (i) They began by meaning simply *poor.* (ii) They went on to mean, *because poor, therefore having no influence or power, or help, or prestige.* (iii) They went on to mean, *because having no influence, therefore downtrodden and oppressed by men.* (iv) Finally, they came to describe *the man who, because he has no earthly resources whatever, puts his whole trust in God."* So in Hebrew the word "poor" came to describe the humble and helpless individuals who put their whole trust in God.

The paradox of poverty, according to Jesus, is that from God's perspective we are wealthiest when we are poor breathers. Material wealth, political prominence, Hollywood stardom, or association with those who have attained these goals will not make us happy or help us gain the kingdom of God. To achieve a deeper knowledge of God, to reach the place of being conscious of nothing except our need for God's love and forgiveness, we must pass through the lonely and dark valleys of soul poverty and self-denial of all things. Only the one who finds his or her pride so shattered so that there is nothing and no one else to trust in but Jesus Christ will find the real rock of happiness that provides the foundation that nothing can shake.

Only those who get on their knees before the cross of Calvary will be able to look up and see the amazing wonder of God's grace. The blessed ones who come to possess the kingdom are, according to A. W. Tozer, those who have learned to repudiate every external thing and have all sense of possessing rooted from their hearts. Only as we admit that we are powerless are we able to attain the kingdom of God, "for power is perfected in weakness" (2 Cor. 12:9).

Jesus announced that these powerless poor breathers who put their whole trust in God would receive abundant grace. To them belonged the entire, limitless kingdom of heaven.

While He sought to give His hearers a right conception of His kingdom and His own character, He did not directly attack the errors of the people. He saw the misery of the world resulting from sin, yet He did not overwhelm them with their wretchedness. Instead, "He taught them of something infinitely better than they had known. Without combating their ideas of the kingdom of God, He told them the conditions of entrance therein, leaving them to draw their own conclusions as to its nature. The truths He taught are no less important to us than to the multitude that followed Him. *We no less than they need to learn these foundation principles of the kingdom of God*" (*The Desire of Ages,* p. 299; italics supplied).

Happy are those who realize their poverty and are able and willing to go to God as beggars. He will not just give them the answer to their immediate need, but will grace them with every asset of His kingdom.

Are you unhappy—paralyzed by fear? Fear of failure? Fear of rejection? Fear of being alone? Fear of not making it on your own after a death or divorce? Fear of being caught and exposed? Fear of God's call to walk an unknown path?

I am reminded of a story about a thief whom an elderly woman caught red-handed. One evening, as she returned home from a church service, she was surprised to find a burglar in her home, robbing her of her few treasures and valuables. Being unarmed, with only her Bible and purse in hand, she resorted to the one thing she trusted and shouted "Acts 2:38," which is of course the verse from Peter's sermon at Pentecost that speaks of repentance and baptism.

When the thief heard her words, without turning to look at the speaker he dropped everything, threw his hands up in the air, and stood there trembling while the woman called the police and explained what she had done. The police responded immediately, and when they arrived, they found the thief as the woman had described him, still standing with his back to the door, hands raised above his head, and trembling like a leaf in the wind. The police officer handcuffed him and took him to his car. Just before they drove away, the officer turned to the thief and said, "What kind of burglar are you, standing there trembling before an unarmed, elderly woman when all she said was a verse from Scripture?"

"A verse from Scripture," the burglar exclaimed incredulously. "I was afraid because I thought she said she had an ax and two .38s!"

Fear paralyzes. Humiliating and degrading its victims, it keeps nations armed at ruinous cost, blocks prosperity and happiness, and hinders the spread of light and truth. Fear is the enemy against which there is no weapon—except faith in God. If you are paralyzed by fear, come before God—now. The first step is to "trust in the Lord with all your heart and do not lean on your own understanding" (Prov. 3:5; see also Ps. 26:1).

Immediately follow that trust with action, such as ridding your mind and heart of everything disturbing, especially guilt. Then, when you have cleared your mind of such haunting thoughts, start doing good deeds, especially those you may have attempted before but failed. Soon, with God's help, you will accomplish even the seemingly impossible as you begin to radically define yourself as one beloved and blessed by God. In fact, repeat the words "I am beloved and blessed by God" every waking moment until they replace the old negative thoughts that labeled you as worthless.

Only this kind of active, practiced faith can succeed in overcoming fear, because faith alone keeps those in perfect peace whose minds are focused on Jesus Christ (see Isa. 26:3). So let us imbibe this beatitude as one would medicine for an ailment. Fear is the number one enemy of faith and the source of much unhappiness. I exhort you to take this seriously, because it is to those who are freed from fear, by God's presence and power, that He promises the kingdom of heaven.

Is lust, the persistent pest of this generation, knocking on your door night and day, suggesting that you will be happy if you log on to the unsavory sexual offerings on the Internet, television, and other entertainment media? Chuck Swindoll said that "when Lust suggests a rendezvous, send Jesus Christ as your representative. Have Him inform your unwanted suitor that you want nothing to do with him. . . . Since you and Christ have been united together, you are no longer a slave. . . . Have Christ inform him that the permanent peace and pleasure you are enjoying in your new home with Christ are so much greater than Lust's temporary excitement that you don't need him around any longer to keep you happy" (*Killing Giants, Pulling Thorns,* p. 26).

Are you disillusioned, disappointed, and depressed? Have you lived with the lingering anguish of loneliness? Do you spend silent nights and dreadful days longing for love, forgiveness, and acceptance? Are you filled with resentment and bitterness, those sneaky thieves of happiness? Are you overwhelmed by pain, grief, or guilt in your life? Have you tried everything, but cannot rid yourself of these and other lethal and relentless emotions that are slowly poisoning your spirit?

Remember that the great invisible God who created the earth and all that is in it, especially you, actually listens to every word you say and actually responds to your requests (Isa. 58:9). Most important, God speaks to you passionately and intimately. He wants you to know that He does not just love you—He's wild about you! Listen, He is speaking, poignantly saying to you personally, "You have ravished my heart with one look of your eyes" (S. of Sol. 4:9, NKJV).

The term *ravish* means "to overcome with emotions of joy and or delight; to be unusually attractive, pleasing and striking." God's heart swells with divine emotions of joy and delight for us, His beloved, even while we are sinners becoming saints. I know that many Christians assume that God loves us only when we are obedient. But have you ever stopped to consider how much He adores us even when we come short of His glory, particularly during the times our hearts are sincerely trying to please Him? Listen to my paraphrase of a powerful passage that speaks to this fact: "For while you were still sick, weak, feeble, diseased, impotent, under the power of sin, at the right time Christ died for the ungodly. . . . For while we were still enemies, shaking our fists at God, we were reconciled to God through the death of His Son, much more, having been reconciled, we shall be saved by His life" (Rom. 5:6-10).

The passionate heart of God swells with joy and delight over His beloved even while we are filled with fear, failing, and self-centeredness. So fling yourself on God's mercy. Raise your eyes and hands to heaven with palms open and upturned as the ancient Jews did, and shout to the Lord this simple prayer that only the poor in spirit can say:

"Nothing in my hand I bring,
Simply to Thy cross I cling;
Naked, come to Thee for dress,
Helpless, look to Thee for grace;
Foul, I to the fountain fly;
Wash me, Savior, or I die!"

You can do it anywhere, audibly or silently. Whatever way you choose, just do it! And you've got nothing to lose and everything to gain.

I know that it works for me. Any time that I face fear and misery, I repeat these thoughts, and the sensation immediately evaporates. Instantly I find myself filled with trust in my ever-present, heart-ravished Abba. The pleasure I then experience these awesome words summarize:

"In His [Jesus'] shade I took great delight and sat down, and his fruit was sweet to my taste. He has brought me to his banquet hall, and his banner over me is love. [He sustains] me with raisin cakes, [refreshes] me with apples, because I am lovesick. . . . Let . . . his right hand embrace me" (Song of Sol. 2:3-6).

This strategy may not work for everyone, but perhaps the following suggestions will. The Sociology Department of Duke University discovered that they are good indicators of peace of mind and happiness. Rich-in-spirit, self-centered, egotistical, and materialistic persons are most deficient in these qualities, but the poor in spirit are blessed when they: (1) avoid being suspicious and resentful and exercise more trust and love; (2) try to live in the present, because brooding over past mistakes and experiences creates unhappiness; (3) recognize conditions that cannot be changed and learn how to live with them; (4) cooperate with life instead of frequently running away from it; (5) force themselves to be outgoing with others rather than to retreat, especially during times of emotional distress; (6) refuse to rely on self-pity or to make alibis for their actions, rather facing their responsibilities with grace; (7) cultivate the old-fashioned virtues of love, honor, loyalty, and thrift; (8) do not expect too much of themselves, but learn to recognize the wide gap between what they think they can do and what they can actually accomplish; (9) find something bigger than themselves in which to believe and participate actively; (10) make Jesus Christ the center and circumference of their lives.

Happy are the poor in spirit, who possess nothing. Theirs is the kingdom of heaven.

CHAPTER

A Message for Mourners

"Happy the mourning—because they shall be comforted."
Matthew 5:4, YLT.

I have conducted many funerals in my almost two decades of parish ministry. But no amount of familiarity with grief and acquaintance with mourners prepares you for your own personal encounter with our great enemy, death. I discovered this not long ago when my mother passed away after years of a progressive illness that ended with her falling asleep in the Lord one quiet Sabbath afternoon.

Prior to her death, I told myself that I knew precisely how I would grieve. It definitely would not be dramatic. Nor would I respond as a victim of God's perceived ungraciousness. Instead, I would exhibit the proper decorum required of a pastor (whatever that is) and would not prolong the pain of my family with any emotional outbursts.

I did shed some highly controlled tears when I gave the homily in front of a church filled with family and friends, most of whom had never heard me, or any other woman, preach. I did restrain my sobs at the graveside as I conducted the committal ceremony. I remained strong for my family, especially my son, who seemed to be devastated by his grief. As I had on so many other occasions, I comforted my sister and ministered to my aunts and uncle. But I felt no overpowering sorrow. Soon I even began to believe that I must be among the fortunate few who manage to escape a visit from this unwanted guest named grief. But come it did, with a vengeance that overwhelmed my strength and health for more than a week.

I returned to my office two Mondays after the funeral, which had taken place on Mother's Day, and launched myself into my duties and responsibilities as if I had simply returned from a disappointing vacation. Then it hit me. I began to shiver as if I were suffering from a severe chill. It forced me to bed, a place where no one would ever find me in the daytime under normal circumstances, no matter how bad I felt. For a while I struggled with a variety of physical aches in my stomach and head, but finally I succumbed to the emotional loss that shrouded me as I sank helplessly between the sheets of my bed.

The floodgates of my emotions finally opened, and I sobbed uncontrollably until I slipped into a very restless sleep. I dreamed that Jesus had come to me, as I had seen in a picture of Him in a hospital, leaning over the bed of a patient. He said to me in my dream, "Let Me hold you, My little one." I shrugged free from His touch. Again He reached out, this time taking me in His arms. I hid my face in His chest and listened to the most comforting words I have ever heard. He said, "My little one, you are not acquainted with your own grief. Rest in Me, and let Me comfort you."

I stayed in bed for a week, for that was how long it took me to truly rest in His comfort. Even now I still cry silent tears sometimes when I am driving alone or when I see a photograph of my mother. But as I write this message to mourners, I sense that God has provided an avenue for me to be comforted even more profoundly as He gives me words to comfort you.

The nation of Israel also covered up their desperate need for comfort with spiritual bravado. Theirs was also an unusual situation before the first advent of Christ. While they were not exiled from the Promised Land, as had been many of their forebears, they were nevertheless spiritual exiles, cut off from direct interaction with God. Many had lost heart and, worse still, as the chosen people of God, had lost faith. Skepticism and indifference increased as some began to express doubts as to whether God still cared for His people at all (Mal. 1:2) and whether obedience meant anything to Him (Mal. 2:17; 3:15).

The less scrupulous had already gone beyond questioning and had begun treating any expression or practice of faith with contempt (Mal. 1:14; 3:7-12). The covenant relationship with God no longer seemed to matter, as adultery, perjury, victimization of the underprivileged, and the infiltration of pagan religious practices became accepted norms of behavior. The spiritual leaders either embraced the new trends or tried to ignore them.

Oral prophecy, which had begun a steady decline after Ezekiel, gradually ceased after Joel and Malachi. God seemed to have withdrawn His shekinah (glorious) presence from His chosen people. There were no more angelic appearances, not even a note of condemnation or condolence from Yahweh, during a 400-year period when public opinion regarded all further prophetic predictions as the work of charlatans worthy of death.

Approximately 90 years before the advent of the Messiah God allowed them to be held hostage by a Gentile army. The Romans occupied the Holy Land.

God had warned His people of the consequences of disobedience, but they had ignored Him. Now the fulfillment of His warnings and the accompanying experience overwhelmed them. They were political prisoners in their own land, without even a prophet to encourage and guide them. Many of the people rebelled and, in the words of an earlier period of their history, "did what was pleasing in [their] own eyes" (Judges 17:6). But they all felt abandoned.

But, as always, a small faithful remnant treasured the written Word of God. They sought to understand God's repeated promise of a Messiah who would, they believed, deliver His people from the Romans and restore the direct, divine relationship they had previously enjoyed.

Matthew's Gospel tells how God broke that long silence by sending His Son, Jesus Christ (Immanuel, God with us). But the blindness and indifference of the religious leaders led a majority to reject the Son of David, the King of kings, the promised High Priest forever, because He was born in a stable outside of Bethlehem.

For 30 years Jesus lived among His people in silence, unrecognized as God dwelling among them. But when the *kairos* (i.e., "the appointed time") to begin His ministry came, He lost no time in preaching, teaching, and calling people to repent and return to a personal relationship with God.

That's where we enter the story in Matthew 5 again, especially the short preface to the Sermon on the Mount. "When Jesus saw the crowds, He went up on the mountain; and after He sat down, His disciples came to Him. He opened His mouth and began to teach them" (Matt. 5:1, 2).

Before we examine His message to mourners, we should consider several points in this preamble. Notice the place—a mountain—from which Jesus preached the sermon. Mountains had a sacred meaning to ancient cultures. Many worshiped their gods in high places, from the Middle East to Greece and Rome, from the ziggurats of Babylon to the Mayan temples of Central America.

According to many passages of Scripture, particularly Psalm 121, the Jews believed that mountains were the dwelling place of God. Many important events in the life of Israel had taken place on a mountain. For example, it was on Mount Moriah that the aged Abraham and his only son, Isaac, learned to trust God unconditionally (Gen. 22:1-8). God established His covenant with His newly established nation of Israel on Mount Sinai (Ex. 19:3-20:26). Elijah stood against 850 prophets of Baal on Mount Carmel, and there God rained down fire from heaven to confirm His power (1 Kings 18:20-40). "Zion" was the summit on which Jerusalem was built.

Thus it was on a nameless mountain, not necessarily one of the ancient holy and famous mountains, that Jesus intimated by action what He would later teach plainly: that the hour had come, "and now is, when the true worshipers will worship the Father in spirit and truth, for such people the Father seeks to be His worshipers" (John 4:23). Such were the people Jesus was seeking as He spoke to His disciples and the multitude that day. He delivered His inaugural address, which included the constitution and conditions for entrance and acceptance in the kingdom of grace, on the side of a mountain still unknown even after centuries of archaeological discovery in that region.

Some of the religious leaders and their spies may have noted a few significant distinctions between this day and the one in which Moses received the law. For example, the holy record tells us that the Lord descended on the mountain (Ex. 19:18), but Matthew, who wrote his Gospel to the Jews, pointed out that Jesus "went up on the mountain." God spoke through thunder and lightning when He gave the law to Moses, but now He was speaking through His only begotten Son, "whom He appointed heir of all things, through whom also He made the world" (Heb. 1:2).

When God had issued the law at Sinai He ordered the people to keep their distance, but on this occasion Jesus welcomed the crowds, inviting them to draw near. Except for the fourth and the fifth, all the commands at Sinai began with "Thou shalt not" and made the recipients tremble with fear, but in the Sermon on the Mount Jesus inspired hope by saying, "Happy are you." He distinguished between the rigid application of the law by Jerusalem's religious leaders, and Christianity, in which the Savior draws near to answer even the very basic needs of His people.

The scribes and Pharisees competed vigorously to "sit in Moses' seat," and ruled with corrupted power from a place of comfort and honor in the Temple. Our Lord Jesus Christ, truth personified, found Himself ejected from the synagogue and rejected in His own town. Instead of seeking the seat of honor, He went to an unidentified mountain to ordain and train His disciples and preach the values of the kingdom of grace.

The Jewish custom of the day had teachers sit when teaching (Matt. 26:55) to show that they had the authority to teach. The reference to Jesus' position ("He sat down") intimates something more significant than that He practiced the prevailing practice of His day. Matthew pointed out Jesus' posture to remind us that the Lord, the King of kings, was sitting on His own throne that day to declare the manifesto of His kingdom. It was not a throne made by human design, but one that He had created.

The biblical writer underscored the fact that Jesus "opened His mouth and began to teach." Isn't it strange that he should mention such an apparently trivial piece of information? After all, in order to speak, one must open his or her mouth. So what point was Matthew highlighting in order to help readers better accept and understand the Beatitudes? He was emphasizing the fact that Jesus spoke with an authority infinitely transcending that of the religious leaders.

Jesus may also have appeared to some as a judge about to execute justice when He sat down. When He opened His mouth to teach, not only did everyone clearly understand Him, but it distinguished His teachings from the vain repetition and speculation of the opposing scribes and Pharisees.

Without fear or favor, Jesus openly set forth the realities of a close intimate relationship with His Father in heaven. His teaching astonished the grief-stricken, mourning multitudes suffering from physical, emotional, and spiritual losses, for He taught as one having authority and not as the scribes and Pharisees (Matt. 7:28, 29).

Let us now carefully examine the message "Happy the mourning—because they shall be comforted." Our English word "mourn" means "to feel or express grief or sorrow; to show the customary signs of grief for a death; to murmur mournfully like the mourning dove." The Greek language has several words for "mourn," but Jesus used *pentheo* (to mourn deeply and intensely, to bewail or lament a loss), the word used especially to describe an external manifestation of grief. Classical Greek commonly used this ancient word for grief without violent manifestations. However, it has a variety of applications in the New Testament, such as general grief, sorrow for the death of a loved one, and deep moans for the overthrow of evil systems. Scripture uses it for contrition for sin and the grief for those condoning it, especially those in a local church who show no repentance.

It seems like an oxymoron to associate happiness with mourning. Mourning was a familiar companion of those poor oppressed peasants who followed Jesus to the mountain that day, as it is to us today. It attacked them in their rough beds after a hard day's labor and woke them early in the mornings. Grief slipped into their hearts to haunt them as the heat of day sapped their strength. Mourning was as familiar to them as every breath they breathed. They lived with one loss after another, longing that one day something would finally deliver them from the deadly grip of grief.

No matter how often we grieve, we can never get used to it. Our spirits instinctively shrink from sadness and suffering. As a result, our natural inclination is to seek out people of cheer and joy. No one likes to be around those in a perpetual state of grief. The entertainment industry, businesses, and churches that try to attract large numbers of people build upon the fact that we hate mourning and will do or pay anything to gain a moment of respite from it.

Like us, the multitudes were desperately seeking comfort when they hobbled up the rough side of the mountain to hear Jesus. They clung to their last vestige of hope that He would heal them so that if only in health, if in nothing else, they would have some respite. So when Jesus said that the second most gratifying experience in His kingdom is mourning, and that those who personally participate in it, not just once, but continually, are not only happy but rewarded with the longed-for divine comfort, the paradox Jesus presented must have amazed them. They did not take into consideration that He was establishing a principle based on personal knowledge and experience. He was the "man of sorrows and acquainted with grief" (Isa. 53:3) who came to His own, only to be rejected by them

(John 1:11). One day He would endure the cross and the hostility of sinners (Heb. 12:2, 3). But there was a "joy set before Him" (verse 2) that was also inherent in the promise made to those who mourn.

To their surprise, they discovered that mourning, the thing that they desired most to get rid of from their lives, they now had to keep on embracing in order to be comforted. This is directly opposite to everything the world then and now teaches. If you listen to some of the most popular preachers today, you will find that they expound a name-it, claim-it gospel of riches and righteousness from their influential electronic pulpits. They reach the hearts and homes of millions of grieving people around the world as they promote wealth by any means. Such religious leaders never say that it is OK to grieve in order to be comforted, but rather they leave a clear impression that if God is really with you, you will not mourn.

Recently I saw a documentary about a Florida evangelist who became internationally famous almost overnight. He had vigorously and vociferously protested against a movie entitled *The Last Temptation of Christ,* heralded by many believers as one of Hollywood's most infamous attempts to portray Jesus as a historical figure who was a mere mortal. The evangelist had gathered thousands of protesters at the movie studios, creating more publicity than the producers had ever dreamed of. It triggered a short but aggressive frenzy in the news media, as all the major networks competed to have the minister on their programs. Attracting the attention of studio executives, advertisers, and even nonbelievers, his popularity grew beyond his wildest expectations. Millions of dollars of contributions poured into the coffers of his congregation. He bought more property, built bigger buildings to accommodate the increasing crowds, and began to preach his name-it, claim-it gospel of wealth.

As he grew in national prominence, so also in local popularity. His church attendance increased rapidly, and his financial fortunes bloomed significantly. Politicians courted him for public endorsements, and religious leaders who sought his support wined and dined him. Within a few years he was not only a poster pinup for the name-it, claim-it promises of fame and fortune of those who proclaim a Christ who seems to sell more than He saves, but the minister eventually began to abuse his public trust and power. His marriage began to fail, and, reportedly, he had an affair with the wife of one of his trusted elders and best friends.

When the elder pointed out his misdemeanor, instead of grieving the loss of trust and relationship with Christ the minister decided to have the elder murdered. The person he tried to hire to commit the deed was an undercover agent who had befriended him while secretly investigating his financial activities. The authorities caught the minister red-handed on videotape as he calmly stated where he wanted the bullet fired into the head of his elder and friend, whose wife he lusted after. The same news media that helped him become rich and famous also had a heyday as they exposed his deceit and expressed their disapproval of religious movements.

It is vital that we maintain a correct reading and understanding of the Word of God. He calls His people to participate in a spiritual experience with a suffering Savior who is ever and always ready to comfort those who mourn. Millions grieve today because of broken hearts, blighted hopes, reversal of financial fortunes, or the loss of loved ones. Nothing human guarantees that they will be comforted. However, with the promise in the preceding beatitude, Christ's declaration applies only to the born-again member of the body of Christ.

We know that Jesus comes to every hurting person with His ministry of healing. All we have to do is to receive it by faith. God does not want us to remain pressed down by sorrow or live with broken hearts. He wants us to approach Him in simple faith and permit Him to guide us until we are comforted.

In my Bible study I have discovered three distinct types of mourning mentioned in the Scriptures. The first is a natural mourning everyone experiences over a loss of any kind. The second is a disconsolate, inordinate grief that is deep and cannot be comforted. It is the hopeless remorse of a sinner, such as Judas, that does not lead to repentance, but to rebellion and self-destruction. And the Holy Spirit initiates the third kind as He convicts us of sin (John 16:8, 9). Such mourning consists of true heart sorrow for personal sin against God. Peter experienced it after He denied his Lord. It also causes us to grieve for the sin in our lives as well as that in the lives of others.

The mourning in the second beatitude encompasses this third type of grieving. It represents the experience of a sinner who encounters the living, holy God. Sometimes it expresses itself by tears and wailing, at other times by soul-searching silence. Such grieving constitutes the process of change we call conversion. Conversion releases us from the old life of sin and relieves us of the guilt—if not necessarily the consequences—of our past life. Flowing from a conscience tenderly touched by the Holy Spirit, it mourns past sins and present unworthiness. Furthermore, such grief sympathizes with our Savior's sufferings—not once for all times, but, according to the verb tense, a continuous experience. Scripture says: "For the sorrow that is according to the will of God produces a repentance without regret, leading to salvation" (2 Cor. 7:10).

Death, the devil's dedicated servant, is the number one cause of mourning. It has been said that the statistics on death are quite impressive. One out of every one person dies.

In the time of Jesus wealthy families would hire mourners who took their jobs quite seriously. Such mourners would show up at the home of the deceased properly attired with the appropriate expressions of grief. They would make wailing noises for three days (John 11:31) in the hopes of driving the spirits of the dead back into their bodies so that they could be resurrected.

Even today we mourn with a family over its loss. As a minister I have observed a variety of ways in which we mourn. Some weep silently. Others are racked by heaving sobs and require support lest they collapse. A few may throw themselves on the coffin or grave of the deceased. One woman once threw herself into the open grave, screaming invectives at God. Many internalize their emotions and remain stoic, appearing untouched by their own pain or the grief of others. Whatever the expression, we are all like little children, powerless and defenseless as we mourn the losses we encounter because of sin's presence in our world.

Both personal sins and corporate omissions are a daily source of grief for the believer. The conscious swirling of pride in our hearts, the coldness of love withdrawn when we find ourselves denied the desires of our lustful hearts, and the lack of a rich harvest of the fruit of the Spirit mentioned in Galatians 5:22, 23 should make all of us weep continuously. We should cry out, "Wretched [man/woman] that I am! Who will set me free from the body of this death?" (Rom. 7:24). Nothing or no one but Jesus Christ can comfort our spiritual grief.

And happy is the converted individual who mourns over the sin and suffering of this world. At times I have experienced this. Recently I ran across the story of a 36-year-old mother who systematically drowned her five children, aged 6 months to 7 years. She chased the last child, the 7-year-old, until she caught him. Then she dragged his squirming body to the bathroom to hold him under the same water in which his siblings had suffered a similar fate moments before. A pain that felt like labor pangs ripped through my stomach. Quickly closing the magazine, I threw it in the wastebasket like a filthy rag before I could finish reading the article. It was too painful to imagine the fear and suffering of the children or the state of mind of a mother who would do such a thing.

Immediately I fell to my knees. Jesus promised never to leave us alone, but in His physical absence He said that He would provide us "another Comforter" to be with us forever (John 14:16, KJV). His assurance brought peace to my mind.

"Blessed be the God and Father of our Lord Jesus Christ, the Father of mercies and God of all comfort, who comforts us in all our affliction so that we will be able to comfort those who are in any affliction with the comfort with which we ourselves are comforted by God" (2 Cor. 1:3, 4).

I am sure you have also shared Jesus' heart-wrenching anguish that no language can adequately portray. My friend Christy Robinson, who is childless, said that the account of a severely sexually abused infant recently featured in the local news made her cry. She said that she felt physical pain and wondered why the perpetrators of such horrible crimes get to have children and she doesn't.

What causes you to mourn as you look around this violent world in which we have been called to be witnesses for God?

The Man of Sorrows, our God of salvation, weeps daily, even moment by moment, for those who are lost. He is comforted only as we repent and return to a reconciled relationship with our heavenly Parent. There's a lot of affliction and mourning in the world because of sin, but thanks be to God, divine comfort abounds even more than grief, through the powerful presence of the Holy Spirit.

But no sorrow can be more searing, no grief more gripping, than the mourning that follows the recognition of our own sinfulness. No one's character can be changed, no one can become a new creature in Christ, without first experiencing the death of self. The apostle Paul said that it is necessary for the believer to die daily (1 Cor. 15:31) in the process of sanctification, but nothing compares with the grief of that first separation from the old carnal life as we step into God's kingdom.

I have had the privilege of leading many to accept Jesus Christ as their personal Savior and observed the tremendous mourning that accompanies such surrender. But in my experience none grieved more at that funeral for self than a man whose hardened heart had resisted the call of his Savior for decades. As we fell to our knees and prayed together, he gave his life to the Lord. When he did, he sobbed so bitterly that I thought he was about to have a heart attack. Powerful waves of weeping racked his body. He tried to describe the images he saw of himself, cruelly crucifying the Lord again and again. Words of repentance mingled with vivid confessions of his continued rebellion as the unspeakable tenderness of God drew him to heaven's heart and he realized how sin had separated him from both his Father in heaven and from his family on earth. As he mourned in brokenness of heart he was consoled, not by me, but by Him who said, Happy "are they that mourn, for they shall be comforted."

Those who experience such mourning receive great blessing, because the Holy Spirit, the member of the Holy Trinity who Jesus said would convict the world of sin, fulfills Jesus' promise (John 16:8, 9). The Spirit follows through with the work of grace that may come in the guise of trial, tribulation, or even temptation. Generally, when we are converted, we immediately find ourselves confronted with a variety of trials. More often than not we assume that they result from the harsh handiwork of the enemy. As a result, we have come to despise our adversities as well as the chastening of the Lord. We often faint when rebuked by the Spirit, and bemoan the pressures of Satan more than we praise the Lamb of God for smelting us into refined gold.

Citizens of God's kingdom must learn that greater is He that is in us than he that is in the world (1 John 4:4). We must recognize that trials can lead to such spiritual benefits as the building of our characters and the deepening of our trust. Brennan Manning said that "the story of salvation-history indicates that without exception trust must be purified in the crucible of trial" (*Ruthless Trust: The Ragamuffin's Path to God,* p. 9). Dietrich Bonhoeffer said that when God wants to use a person, He first crushes them.

Although God does not send or initiate life's trials, He does use them as tools to remove the impurities of our lives and to smooth the rough edges in our character. Their hewing, squaring, chiseling, burnishing, and polishing work is a painful process because it presses us hard against the grinding wheel of sanctification. As we endure such experiences we must remember that a jeweler never puts much effort and attention into fool's gold or useless stones. Only gold and valuable gemstones get polished with such persistence. Jesus Christ, the Master Jeweler in whose crown each converted person is set, uses trials and temptations to polish the living stones for the building of His eternal kingdom. So "happy the mourning—because they shall be comforted." Rejoice in hope, for "this is the victory that overcomes the world, our faith" (1 John 5:4, RSV).

There can be no comfort where there is no grief. It is interesting that "comfort" comes from the Greek word *parakaleo,* meaning "to come to one's side, in a personal and intimate fashion; to call to one's aid, to send for, to console, to cheer, to exhort, to encourage." It is also the same word that the New Testament often uses to refer to the "Holy Spirit." Such comfort is one of the specific functions of the Holy Spirit in our world today. It is also the work of the other members of the Trinity in our lives.

Those who mourn under the chastening rod of God find themselves comforted with the peaceful fruit of righteousness from the Father (Heb. 12:11). The one who grieves over the dishonor done to the character of our loving Lord by those who claim to be believers also receives comforting from Jesus Christ. It appears to me that those who have been wounded the most (by what Brennan Manning calls the trinity of pain, suffering, and evil) become the best apostles of the Suffering Servant after conversion. They seem to accept and understand this kind of comforting best. I frequently see this in survivors of sexual, physical, and emotional abuse. In those who have lost loved ones, especially babies, to death. In those who have overcome bitter divorces. And in those who have failed at everything, especially relationships that produced progeny but never led to marriage.

People who have endured such tragic, painful indignities provide the best comfort to those consumed by rage, shame, self-hatred, suicide, or depression and despair. After they have experienced God's healing love, discovered the assurance of His forever friendship and presence (Matt. 28:20), and tasted divine comfort, they praise Him with more energy and serve Him with a deeper commitment than some raised in Christian homes or who have never suffered the harshness of this sinful world.

As we daily experience the free and full forgiveness found only in

Christ Jesus, we experience the unbelievable comfort the Holy Spirit generously pours out upon us. However, the final comfort, the one that is complete and uninterrupted, will come at the end of this evil age. It will be ours when we at last leave this world. Thankfully, though, we can begin to taste it here and now in the wonderful work of the Holy Spirit, who causes sorrow to flee.

Those who trust God despite difficulty, despair, and disappointment—even continuous mourning—will be made happy in Jesus, the great Comforter of all pain and suffering. " 'Comfort, O comfort My people,' says your God. 'Speak kindly to Jerusalem; and call out to her, that her warfare has ended, that her iniquity has been removed, that she has received of the Lord's hand double for all her sins' " (Isa. 40:1, 2).

Double mourning? Double punishment? Double what we deserve for our sins? Yes, but not only that—praise God, there is also double comfort! The Lord started by saying, "Comfort, O comfort." And we receive it from the Lord's own hand. "He will wipe away every tear from [our] eyes" (Rev. 21:4). Tenderly He wipes away every tear.

Lord, "you've kept track of [our] every toss and turn through the sleepless nights, each tear entered in your ledger, each ache written in your book. . . . God, you did everything you promised, and I'm thanking you with all my heart. You pulled [us] from the brink of death, [our] feet from the cliff-edge of doom. Now [we] stroll at leisure with God in the sunlit fields of life" (Ps. 56:8-13, Message).

The world is wrapped up in grief, but God said, "Happy the mourning—because they shall be comforted." He also added in another place: " 'For I know the plans that I have for you,' declares the Lord, 'plans for welfare and not calamity to give you a future and a hope' " (Jer. 29:11).

That makes me happy right now, doesn't it you? There's more to come. Read on!

CHAPTER

Meek? Who, Me? You've Got to Be Kidding!

"Happy the meek—because they shall inherit the [earth]."
Matthew 5:5, YLT.

The third beatitude is perhaps the most challenging of all. Even the average reader will be struck by the fact that meekness, or gentleness, is by no means a blessing in our world today. The last thing anyone would like to be characterized as is "meek." Most of us think of ourselves as spirited people who know how to stand up for ourselves and our rights. As the old saying goes, we "don't take things lying down." After all, we live in a world that regards the aggressive and assertive as the only winners. We know of no truly meek persons who have inherited anything, especially a piece of the earth, and were able to hold on to it for long. A sensitive, meek, and gentle spirit is the worst equipment for the battle of life when the prizes go to the swift and the wreaths of victory to the bold.

For instance, a missionary was instructing a Hindu student in the Beatitudes. He attempted to explain the meaning and blessing of meekness by pointing to the pious demeanor of another English missionary. Midway through the monologue the student interrupted and said, "Sir, the Englishman may inherit the earth, but if you called him meek to his face, he would be highly insulted."

In our mind the meek always come in last. Leonard Bernstein once remarked in a television documentary that it is practically impossible to find anyone who is willing to play the second chair of any instrument. "I can get plenty of first violinists," he observed, "but to find one who plays *second* violin with as much enthusiasm, or *second* French horn or *second* flute—now, that's a problem. And yet, *if no one plays second, we have no harmony."*

Anyone, especially the secular, postmodern men and women of our day, would take umbrage with Jesus' claim that the meek—the perceived second fiddle—are happy and that they, of all people, will inherit the earth.

In his book *When God Was Man* J. B. Phillips presented the following parody of the Beatitudes that seems to fit the demeanor of our day.

"Happy are the 'pushers': for they get on in the world.

"Happy are the hard-boiled: for they never let life hurt them.

"Happy are they who complain: for they get their own way in the end.

"Happy are the blasé: for they never worry over their sins.

"Happy are the slave drivers: for they get results.

"Happy are the knowledgeable men of the world: for they know their way around.

"Happy are the troublemakers: for they make people take notice of them" (pp. 26, 27).

Aristotle, the Greek philosopher, once said that the virtue of meekness does not lie in the mean between two opposite vices. He insisted that this virtue, if we could even call it that, leans toward the defect that demonstrates a want of sensibility or perception and is a slavish thing that demands a person take insults calmly.

In *War of the Worlds* H. G. Wells scornfully commented on what he regarded as a marked characteristic of meekness. He said that the "meek" are people who are no good, have no spirit in them, possess no proud dreams, and experience no proud lusts. To him, they were nothing but "funk and precautions."

Chuck Swindoll suggested that when many of us read that the meek shall inherit the earth, we "immediately . . . get a false impression. We think, 'Blessed are the weak, for they shall become doormats.' In our rough-and-rugged individualism, we think of gentleness as weakness, being soft, and virtually spineless" (*Improving Your Serve,* p. 104).

So what did Jesus mean when He made this unusual declaration? Why did He challenge believers to follow Him, using the word "meek" to describe His own disposition? He said, "Take My yoke upon you and learn from Me, for I am *gentle [meek]* and humble in heart, and you will find rest for your souls" (Matt. 11:29).

When the apostle Matthew tried to describe the promised Messiah in his Gospel, written specifically to Jews, he quoted the prophet Zechariah. "Say to the daughter of Zion, 'Behold your King is coming to you, *gentle [meek],* and mounted on a donkey, even on a colt, the foal of a beast of burden'" (Matt. 21:5; cf. Zech. 9:9).

What exactly does it mean to be meek or gentle, especially since Scripture says that meekness should be the adornment of the Christian? The apostle Peter cautioned that our "adornment must not be *merely* external—braiding the hair, and wearing gold jewelry, or putting on dresses" (1 Peter 3:3). Instead, said he, "let it be the hidden person of the heart, with the imperishable quality of a *gentle [meek]* and quiet spirit, which is precious in the sight of God" (verse 4). Peter also commented that the quality of meekness is a willingness and ability to take wrong patiently while being gentle and compassionate with others (1 Peter 2:19-25). More than any other follower of Jesus, he had learned, the hard way, repeatedly and painfully, that meekness is the only answer to the eternal human quest and question "How can I inherit the earth?"

Bible students have had considerable differences of opinion as to exactly what "meek" really means, as well as how such a person should behave. Some have proposed that it describes a believer who is weak, listless, and basically a wimp. Such an interpretation has led many into a false understanding of exactly who they are or should be as Christians. It causes some, especially among the ultraconservatives, to become pious doormats who embrace unnecessary indignities to express an attitude of what many describe as the "worm theology," based on one verse they often recite from Psalm 22. There, as David agonized over his plight, he exclaimed, "But I am a worm and not a man, a reproach of men and despised by the people" (verse 6). Obviously David was describing the treatment he was receiving from his persecutors more than making a statement about his self-worth and esteem.

It is important to note that God has never made a human worm, and at no time, even when ravaged by the depravity of sin, is a human described in His Word as a worm! We are sons and daughters of God made in His image and redeemed by the blood of our *magnalia dei,* majestic God, Jesus Christ our Lord. "Meekness should not be confused with weakness," declared George Knight, who also added, "The strength of the meek is accompanied by humility and a genuine dependence on God" (*The Abundant Life Bible Amplifier—Matthew,* p. 85).

Other scholars emphasize the fact that the Greek term *praos,* "meek," is equivalent to the Hebrew word *ani,* which means "poor, weak, afflicted, or humble." It describes those who, like many in the multitude to whom Jesus spoke these words, suffer from some kind of physical disability or material distress.

The English word "humble," sometimes used interchangeably with "meek," is rooted in the concept of freedom from pride and self-assertiveness. In fact, it comes from the Latin *humus,* which means "earth, soil, dirt." This meaning in no way suggests that in order to be humble we must become like dirt, but simply signifies that we are all cut from the same clay as descendants of Adam and Eve.

Further study of the use of the word "meek" in Scripture reveals that it is generally linked and cannot be separated from lowliness, i.e., a humble manner and attitude (Matt. 11:29; Eph. 4:2). Since our English meaning for "lowliness" is the quality or state of being modest or of low economic and social rank, many Christians regard wealth with a jaundiced, suspicious eye. They support their attitude with the idea that Jesus was born of a poor family in Nazareth and never garnered wealth for Himself; therefore, that provides His claim to be meek and humble.

To be meek, however, is not about status in life. It is rather about how we esteem ourselves in terms of others, as the apostle Paul recommends. "Do not merely look out for your own personal interests, but also for the interests of others," he declared (Phil. 2:4). He then exhorts believers:

"Have this attitude in yourselves which was also in Christ Jesus, who, although He existed in the form of God, did not regard equality with God a thing to be grasped, but emptied Himself, taking the form of a bond-servant, and being made in the likeness of men [a powerful allusion to the clay from which humanity is cut]. Being found in appearance as a man, He *humbled* Himself by becoming obedient to the point of death, even death on a cross" (Phil. 2:5-8).

Did you know that Scripture intimately associates the word "meek" with the word "gentle"? (See 2 Cor. 10:1, 2 and Titus 3:2.) English dictionaries describe gentleness as mildness of manners or a kind, amiable disposition. Some people interpret this to mean that anyone who is soft-spoken and shy is a gentle person. Some pious people try to impress others by falsely manifesting such characteristics even when their hearts and minds are boiling over with hostility.

I once knew a man so soft-spoken that we would have to ask him repeatedly, "What did you say?" He would hardly raise his voice in church because he wanted to impress others as to how gentle he was. Yet on one occasion when I happened on him interacting with his wife outside the church, I was shocked to hear him bellowing loudly and venomously at a decibel level that could be heard far across the parking lot. He was screaming and yelling humiliating invectives to that poor woman.

He obviously did not understand the meaning of the word "gentle." Many have forgotten that the original English meaning comes from the word "gentry," describing someone belonging to a family of high social and economic status and who is always appropriate in manners and behavior, both privately and publicly.

It has been said that "if we possess the humility of our Master, we shall rise above the slights, the rebuffs, the annoyances, to which we are daily exposed, and they will cease to cast a gloom over the spirit." Why? Because "the highest evidence of nobility in a Christian is self-control" (*The Desire of Ages,* p. 301).

The word "meek," or gentle, is also closely associated with self-control, a condition of mind and heart that greatly influences one's behavior. Vine's *Expository Dictionary of New Testament Words* tells us that "in its use in Scripture, in which it has a fuller, deeper significance than in nonscriptural Greek writings, [gentleness] consists not in a person's 'outward behavior only; nor in his relations to his fellow-men; as little in his mere natural disposition. Rather it is an inwrought grace of the soul; and the exercises of it are first and chiefly towards God. It is that temper of spirit in which we accept His dealings with us as good, and therefore without disputing or resisting; it is closely linked with the word *tapeinophrosune* [humility], and follows directly upon it, Ephesians 4:2; Colossians 3:12. . . . It is only the humble heart which is also the meek, and which, as such, does not fight against God and more or less struggle and contend with Him. This meekness, however, being first of all a meekness before God, is also such in the face of men, even of evil men, out of a sense that these, with the insults and injuries which they may inflict, are permitted and employed by Him for the chastening and purifying of His elect' " (pp. 55, 56).

In his book *Improving Your Serve* Chuck Swindoll noted that the word "gentle," or meek, "is used several ways in extrabiblical literature" as follows:

"A wild stallion that has been tamed, brought under control, is described as being 'gentle.'

"Carefully chosen words that soothe strong emotions are referred to as 'gentle' words.

"Ointment that takes the fever and sting out of a wound is called 'gentle.'

"In one of Plato's works, a child asks the physician to be tender as he treats him. The child uses the term 'gentle.'

"Those who are polite, who have tact and are courteous, and who treat others with dignity and respect are called 'gentle' people" (pp. 104, 105).

The people who are meek in this sense will and do inherit the earth. They own and enjoy it. The word "inherit" comes from *kleronomeo.* A conjoined word, when separated it means to obtain or receive something by lot *(kleros),* and to possess or receive something as one's own *(nemomai).* In the New Testament it took on a broader significance to include all spiritual good provided through and in Jesus Christ, particularly everything contained in the hope grounded in the promises of God. Scripture uses *kleronomeo* to describe the following:

- A birthright that one enjoys, not because of a price paid or a task accomplished, but by virtue of sonship (Gal. 4:30 and Heb. 1:4; 12:17).
- That which one receives as a gift of grace through the exercise of faith and patience, in contrast with that of a reward resulting from keeping the law (Heb. 1:14; 6:12).
- That which one obtains on the condition of obedience to certain precepts of God (1 Peter 3:9) and faithfulness to God amid severe persecution and opposition (Rev. 21:7).
- The reward of eternal life in this and the coming age by those who acknowledge the supremacy of Christ in this life (Matt. 19:29).
- The reward of those who have shown kindness to followers of the Lord during times of distress (Matt. 25:34-36).
- The kingdom to which it is impossible for sinners to attain (1 Cor. 15:50).

And last, but not least:

- The reward of the soul that forbears retaliation and self-vindication, choosing instead to express itself in gentleness of behavior, as Jesus described in Matthew 5:5.

The word for earth, in this verse, is *tein gein,* the same word the Septuagint employed to describe the arable land that God created out of nothing in the beginning (Gen. 1:1), as well as the material from which He fashioned the first man and woman (Gen. 2:7). It depicts the inhabited world over which God gave authority to the first couple to rule, prior to sin (Gen. 1:26-28).

The ones who will "inherit" are the heirs, born-again believers, children of God in concert with Jesus Christ (Rom. 8:17). They have received every lovely thing created by God. His meek heirs are not annoyed or grieved by the fact that some things belong to others. They possess a lightness of heart, a thrill for living in spite of the sordid limitations and self-imposed restraints of those who refuse to accept the abundant grace of God. Nothing or no one can break the joy or dispossess the meek or gentle, because they believe that they "can do *all things* through Him [Christ] who strengthens" them (Phil. 4:13).

If you are not yet persuaded that God's promise to the meek has unlimited resources, power, and authority in it, let us examine the lives of some of the truly meek and gentle men and women in the Bible. The first person who comes to mind is Moses. One of the most fiery-tempered people in the Bible, he lost his temper with people and, in one case, murdered a man in a fit of anger (Ex. 2:11, 12). Sometimes he expressed extreme frustration with God and outrage with the children of Israel that the Lord had called him to lead them to the Promised Land. Remember the incident, reported in Exodus 32, when he came down from Mount Sinai and found that during his absence the people had made a golden calf and worshiped it? After he had talked God out of His anger toward the people because of their idolatrous acts (verses 11-14), Moses lost his temper with them over the same issue.

When he saw that the people had not followed the instructions he had left them, he became so angry that for a moment he forgot what he had in his hands—the sacred tables of stone on which God with His own finger had written the Ten Commandments. He became so outraged, especially when he spotted the golden calf and the people dancing and worshiping before it, that, as the Bible reports it, "Moses' anger *burned,* and he *threw* the tablets from his hands and *shattered them* at the foot of the mountain" (verse 19). In order to have "shattered" them, he had to fling the sacred tables of stone (not thin slate) to the ground with violent rage. Yet, to my surprise (and perhaps yours), when a biblical writer later described him, he wrote, "Now the man *Moses was very humble [meek], more than any man who was on the face of the earth"* (Num. 12:3). Why? Because he trusted God implicitly and believed that as His child, he owned and enjoyed everything. To this day, when we want to illustrate this character trait, some Christians say that one has to be "as meek as Moses."

Another meek person was Deborah, the only recorded female judge in the history of ancient Israel. Her name means "a bee." She was, to paraphrase the words of Muhammad Ali, "as gentle as a butterfly, but stung like a bee." The Spirit of God was strong in her life. A highly charismatic character, she bore the title of "prophetess" (Judges 4:4).

Deborah served as judge at a time when the Israelites again endured extreme distress, suffering from the constant military raids of a neighboring nation. Israel's leaders seemed to have exhausted all means of resistance. Their princes had been captured and were now slaves. The poor people had been dispersed, and the nation was desperate when God turned to this woman to deliver them. God's instrument to rescue His people, she was not afraid to speak divine words with authority. Skilled in leadership, she demonstrated the kind of wisdom that caused the great of her nation to seek her advice as she sat under a palm tree, her court or judgment seat. As Deborah rallied and unified the scattered tribes of Israel she preached courageously and prophetically and humbly accepted the mantle of leadership in a story that is a powerful, encouraging message to the meek.

But no one will ever be able to surpass the meekness of Jesus Christ, the God-man who described Himself as gentle and humble (Matt. 11:29). Truly He could say, "Blessed are the meek: for they shall inherit the earth" (KJV), because, although mocked, derided, and spat upon, still He did not retaliate or rage against His abusers.

Could there be a more treacherous scene in human history than when a trusted disciple tried to cover up his dastardly deed with a friendly greeting and a kiss of welcome? Yet Jesus did not strike Judas or fling him to the ground in anger. Instead, He welcomed him, saying, "Friend, do what you have come for" (Matt. 26:50).

Jesus was unjustly accused and dishonestly condemned, yet even then His silence astonished Pilate, who asked, "'Do You not hear how many things they testify against You?' And He [Jesus] did not answer him with regard to even a *single* charge, so the governor was quite amazed" (Matt. 27:13, 14).

When His own people rejected Him and His own friends forsook Him and fled, still He uttered no reproach. As Peter denied Him not once but three times, Jesus turned and looked at him with such passionate love that it redeemed the wretched man and restored his confidence and trust in God. It transformed Peter into one of the greatest of apostles.

On the cross Jesus exclaimed, "Father, forgive them; for they do not know what they are doing" (Luke 23:34).

Make no mistake—Jesus was not a wimp. Encountering the cruelty and injustice done to others, particularly the underdogs of His day, He experienced and demonstrated intense anger. He responded with rage to the debasement of His Father's house (Matt. 21:12, 13). When the scribes and Pharisees objected to Jesus' healing suffering and illness on the Sabbath, He defied them and did exactly that in their presence (Luke 6:1-11). But although self-satisfaction might upset Him, when the pious religious rulers tried to entrap Him in His words, He remained calm (Mark 12:13-40).

Even the best of us, when confronted with someone deliberately maligning our character, become defensive. If they try to lure us into compromising statements, to say something rash that they may use against us, as soon as we are aware of their plot we become angry or boil with resentment. Not so with Jesus! Some of the noblest answers ever given and recorded in Scripture were responses to questions asked with the express intention of entrapping Him.

The secret of His calmness under such duress is that Jesus never felt any kind of animosity or indignation toward anything done to or against His own person. Unlike sinners, He was never eager to vindicate Himself, especially immediately after an accusation. He never exercised His "right" or exhibited the arrogant and aggressive attitude that He "owed it to Himself to look out for Number One." Instead He surrendered all to His heavenly

Father, who said: *"Vengeance is Mine, I will repay"* (Rom. 12:19). He gave everything (emptying Himself [Phil. 2:7]) for the salvation of men and women until nothing remained to take care of Jesus, the man from Nazareth. So also should those who aspire to be meek and desire to inherit the earth be like Jesus.

Meekness, or gentleness, according to the words and life of Jesus, must include the ability to have tremendous strength under control. Only then can we be calm and peaceful when a sudden storm sweeps us away like a feather in a tornado. It is to be grateful in the midst of adversity, particularly when it is not of our own making.

Instead of emitting toxic fumes of fury that permanently poison relationships, we are to respond with soothing, tactful, and gracious words that preserve the self-esteem and dignity of even our opponents. Thus we give our enemies a way out—and perhaps a way back into grace—even while establishing that they are wrong. It means to esteem the boundaries of others with courtesy, respect, and honor while not allowing them to tear down our own.

A meek person is one who has unlimited authority and resources, but restrains and holds them under control. However, most of us are more like Peter before his conversion: proud, impetuous, and hungry for power. He made promises that he couldn't keep (John 13:37) and was a controlling person who thought he knew better than even Jesus, to the point of rebuking Him (Mark 8:32). Also he struggled with the obsession for revenge (Matt. 18:21). Under certain circumstances his great passion led him to take greater risks than the others took to be with Jesus (Matt. 14:29). So how does a truly converted person who struggles with such extremes while desperately desiring to inherit the earth find the balance to become meek?

Many Christian psychologists conclude that meekness is a learned behavior. A study of Scriptures, however, suggests that it is a gift of the Holy Spirit expressed in the words and practiced through the deeds of a believer. Henry Cloud, Christian psychologist, radio personality, and coauthor of the best seller *Boundaries,* suggests that in order to be meek, we need to combine both concepts. He said that under the power of the Holy Spirit, we must learn to restrain aggressive urges to control, cease to seek revenge against those who have hurt us, and practice overcoming the tendency to "annihilate" others.

The first step toward becoming meek, so that the powerful promise of Jesus may be fulfilled in our lives, is to surrender to God. This is how we become poor in spirit. We experience a sense of our own insufficiency, a realization of our own unworthiness and unprofitableness as we crave God's presence. A desire for fulfillment compels us to cry out daily to God, saying, "Please help me!" It is a "lowliness of heart . . . the strength that gives victory to the followers of Christ; it is the token of their connection with the courts above" (*The Desire of Ages,* p. 301).

Jesus said, "If anyone wishes to come after Me, he must deny himself, and take up his cross and follow Me" (Mark 8:34). Here we find the second step toward attaining the meekness that will make us happy inheritors of the earth.

According to A. W. Tozer, Christ summons us to acknowledge and repudiate self and to consider it crucified with Christ. Mark 8:34 calls us to renounce self, which Tozer describes as an "opaque veil that hides the face of God from us" through a variety of self-sins (*The Pursuit of God,* p. 44). He listed "the self-sins" as "self-righteousness, self-pity, self-confidence, self-sufficiency, self-admiration, self-love and a host of others like them" (p. 43). These, he suggested, "dwell too deep within us and are too much a part of our natures to come to our attention till the light of God is focused upon them" *(ibid.).*

Tozer believes that "the grosser manifestations of these sins—egotism, exhibitionism, self-promotion—are strangely tolerated in Christian leaders, even in circles of impeccable orthodoxy. They are so much in evidence as actually, for many people, to become identified with the gospel" *(ibid.).* He also observed that "promoting self under the guise of promoting Christ is currently so common as to excite little notice" and said that "self can live unrebuked at the very altar. It can watch the bleeding Victim die and not be in the least affected by what it sees. It can fight for the faith of the reformers and preach eloquently the creed of salvation by grace and gain strength by its efforts. To tell the truth, it seems actually to feed upon orthodoxy and is more at home in a Bible conference than in a tavern. Our very state of longing after God may afford it an excellent condition under which to thrive and grow" (*ibid.,* pp. 43, 44).

The self-life is such a powerful force that only radical surgery performed by the Holy Spirit can eliminate its presence and eradicate its influence. When this occurs, it is always accompanied by a deep sense of mourning over our lost condition, not simply because some of our rebellious acts bring unpleasant consequences, but because we suddenly become painfully aware that every sin wounds Jesus. We profoundly realize that they disconnect us from a personal relationship with our heavenly Father. Only as we grasp what the unrepudiated self-life does to us, that it sometimes leads to unspeakable ordeals of suffering, can we deny it. As we recognize that in some measure it is like the affliction through which our Savior passed under Pontius Pilate to set us free from the power, presence, and penalty of sin, we become less slaves to self.

Finally, after we have passed through this humbling process, we begin to develop and practice the spirit of meekness imparted by the Holy Spirit. Jesus declared that the Holy Spirit is a meek member of the Godhead (John 16:5-15). He never speaks on His own initiative, but always testifies of Christ as He convicts us of sin, guides us into life eternal, and discloses what is to come so that we may glorify God.

Such meekness is not a fractured spirit, but a surrendered, receptive, obedient, and teachable attitude that follows a broken and contrite heart (Ps. 51:17). The antithesis of pride, stubbornness, fierceness, and vengeance, it helps us grow into the likeness of Christ as a new creature (see Rom. 6).

Meekness is not a natural human attribute, as is pride, its vicious opponent. Nor is it the false piousness that sometimes appears among Christians. Such pretentious meekness never seems to have the guts just to say no and stand for what is right no matter what the opposition or the cost. Rather, it leads to criminal behavior in the ungodly and impetuous acts with grievous consequences in believers.

The meekness that God blesses and that leads to happiness is not inherent in human nature, but comes only as a gift. It is not self-developed, but is divinely imparted and operated. It is the learned surrender of all of the power of the wild stallion of sin to Jesus Christ, who promised that happy "are the meek, for they shall inherit the earth" (NKJV).

Anyone, even those with the most violent tempers or impulsive dispositions, can be transformed into meekness by beholding Jesus and becoming changed into His likeness. Comfortable in our own skin, we will then never hurt others by word or deed. It is being able to forgive ourselves consistently and others constantly. And it is being able to love one another, just as Jesus Christ our Lord has loved us (see John 15:12).

Scripture makes many promises to the meek (for examples, see Psalm 22:26; 25:9; 76:9; 147:6 149:4; Isaiah 29:19; 61:1). We find countless other beautiful promises buried in the Word of God. As a matter of fact, when Jesus said, "Happy [are] the meek," for "they shall inherit the [earth]," He was actually echoing Psalm 37:11, which says, "But the humble [meek] will inherit the land and will delight themselves in abundant prosperity."

Psalm 37:11 was a familiar promise to which the ancient people of God clung, especially the landless, marginalized poor. It embodied all the hopes of inheriting the Promised Land made to their foreparents at the time of the Exodus. The concept was as significant to them as the dream of owning a piece of the rock is to Americans today. But they also knew what many of us are only finally learning—that aggressively seeking material dreams does not make one happy or blessed.

Jesus was pointing them to a more permanent Promised Land. His was an Old Testament promise with a New Testament meaning, because the land of Canaan they entered after the Exodus was but a mere symbol of the real inheritance. It was the invisible kingdom of God for now, but when Christ returns, it will be a re-created earth restored to the beauty it had before the advent of sin.

Christ knew that abiding happiness can exist only in a world without sin. Nothing can achieve it in the present life. As long as sin abounds, no amount of worldly goods or numbers of friends can make us permanently happy and prosperous. If you doubt this, ask the Kennedy family of Massachusetts. Their family has boasted some of the greatest leaders in the world, including a president, a U.S. attorney general, a senator, and many other elected local officials. However, their vast wealth could not stay the trauma and tragic sufferings caused by assassinations, accidents, and other tragedies.

When Jesus said, Happy "are the meek, for they shall inherit the earth," it was a summons to "buy from Me gold refined by fire so that you may become rich" (Rev. 3:18) in His eternal Promised Land. He wanted His listeners who sought the benefits of His kingdom without accepting His blood to know that He is the only way to inherit and own the earth.

An inheritance can only be given in a "will and testament" before the death of the one who bequeaths it and received only after the death of the giver. The Creator and owner of the earth (Ps. 24:1, 2), Jesus died for the sin of the world, but before He did, He said, "They shall inherit the earth."

Jesus took an old promise and made it new. The inheritance of the meek definitely did not involve this world darkened by sin and the shadow of death, in which the rich get wealthier and the poor die wanting. Rather, it is the kingdom described by the prophet Isaiah (cf. Isa. 49:10, 11) that is our hope. Only there with God will we never experience disappointment, sorrow, sickness, grief, or death.

In addition to the literal aspect of this promise, we must not forget its spiritual dimension. According to Genesis 1:28-31, God gave Adam and Eve dominion over the earth. But they chose to disobey God, and their sin caused them to forfeit those rights for themselves and their descendants. Jesus Christ regained it for all the meek—the kingdom dwellers who have nothing, yet possess all things by the grace of God (1 Cor. 3:21, 22).

As God delivers us from our greedy, grasping dispositions, we become content in whatever circumstances we find ourselves (Phil. 4:11). Decades ago, when I was immersed in the political world, I plotted and schemed and manipulated people and situations to possess my part of the great American dream. I felt it was my inalienable right to own a home. Before long I did— but discovered that it actually owned me, as I became a prisoner to its demands. It decided when I could go on vacation and how much I could spend on food, clothes, and recreational activities.

But when I became converted and obeyed God's instructions to get rid of my idols, especially that home, I felt like a caged bird that had finally escaped its prison. After overcoming the initial pain that all addicts experience when breaking the chains of addiction to "thingdom," I had a tremendous sense of relief! I had nothing. I owned nothing. Yet for the first time in my life I was happy. No longer was I depressed and suicidal.

Learning that "better is the little of the righteous than the abundance of many wicked" (Ps. 37:16), I discovered contentment of mind and spirit that has stayed with me and increased as my relationship with Christ has deepened. In the end, my friends—those who knew the old me—joined with those who now share the abundant happiness of inheriting the earth in making the same observation about me that was said of Job. They declare (too often for my comfort level) that "the end of Hyveth Williams is much better than her beginning!"

After reading my autobiography, *Will I Ever Learn?* one friend said that she wouldn't have chosen me as a friend in those preconversion days. But she's seen the miraculous transformation that the Holy Spirit has accomplished in my life. She knows that even though He is not through with me yet, He is emptying me of self so as to make room for the Holy Spirit.

No matter what your lot or situation, do not despair over the apparent prosperity of the wicked while you are poor in material resources. Just stop for a moment and read the words of Asaph (Ps. 73).

David, the great king whose life at times was a type of Christ, said:

"Wait for the Lord and keep His way, and He will exalt you to inherit the land; when the wicked are cut off, you will see it. I have seen a wicked, violent man spreading himself like a luxuriant tree in its native soil. Then he passed away, and lo, he was no more; I sought for him, but he could not be found. Mark the blameless man, and behold the upright; for the man of peace will have a posterity. But transgressors will be altogether destroyed; the posterity of the wicked will be cut off. But the salvation of the righteous is from the Lord; He is their strength in time of trouble" (Ps. 37:34-39).

The humble Christian is far happier in a poor house than in a palace of wickedness (Ps. 84:10 and Prov. 15:16). It is not the proud or the rich and famous but the meek who have appropriated this divine grace to themselves.

Are you ready to drop self-conceit and self-sufficiency and be meek? By God's grace, I am! Won't you join me? You see, it's not only misery that loves company. We formerly selfish, arrogant, and conceited individuals now undergoing the change of life in Christ desperately need the company of God's committed disciples.

Happy are the meek, for *they* shall inherit (and keep on inheriting) the earth!

CHAPTER

5

I Can't Get Any Satisfaction!

"Happy those hungering and thirsting for righteousness—because they shall be filled." Matthew 5:6, YLT.

I was in a hotel lobby when it caught my attention. An oversized poster depicted a man bending forward so that a huge dog could reach him and lick his face with a long, slobbery tongue. His features were a picture postcard of contentment. Behind him stood a woman whose face was a caricature of consternation. Her mouth was contorted with exasperation. The caption at the bottom of the poster declared, "We will never make some people happy. To all others we guarantee satisfaction."

I guess I'm among the ones represented by that shocked woman. One of the worst things in the world to me is a dog that sniffs in embarrassing places and licks one's face with a sloppy tongue. Perhaps my problem is that I am a cat woman. I can't imagine any finicky feline (and they all are that at one time or another) slobbering over anyone, even a beloved owner, the way a dog does. They may lick our hands or feet, or even give a love bite, but drool over our faces? Never!

I suppose I'm sometimes as finicky as a cat myself. So maybe that's why, in the unforgettable words from the song by the now-aging Rolling Stones, "I can't get no satisfaction."

No one disagrees with Maslow's theory of the innate hierarchy of human needs that places food and water as the first and foremost necessities of life. Extreme hunger, thirst, and other unsatisfied desires are among the most disturbing aspects of our personal lives.

From the moment of birth our need for adequate nutrition is immediate, and if, for any reason, we cannot satisfy our hunger and thirst, we won't develop into fully functioning individuals. So urgent are these drives that we cannot wait to be fed. Thus modern society has created a vast network of restaurants and fast-food outlets to accommodate our needs.

In the beginning of human history Eve may not have been hungry for food or thirsty for drink, but it appears that an unsatisfied psychological desire for knowledge drove her to succumb to the devil's temptation. She willingly forfeited Paradise to satisfy an unholy urge (Gen. 3). And guess what the wily one used to tempt her? The need for food. Generations later, when Esau was also hungry, he sold his birthright for a bowl of red lentil soup, also to satisfy the pangs of desire (Gen. 25:29-34).

Before I became a Christian I was famished and thirsty, but not for food and drink and especially not for righteousness. Craving fame and fortune, I was willing to sell my soul to anyone—including the devil—to acquire riches and notoriety. (Have you noticed how we seldom hear of anyone who would sell their soul for righteousness and its eternal rewards?) Many people are still hungry and sell themselves out to the enemy, even though what they gain provides at best only temporary satisfaction.

I belong to a generation that has worked hard to make sure that it has little time for silent reflection, few moments of hunger, and no pangs of thirst. If you doubt this, check out the media systems, fast-food restaurants, and bottling companies that we've turned into billion-dollar industries. We don't want to be driven by such cravings. It therefore bothers me that Jesus sets His seal of approval on the importance of hunger and thirst for righteousness when I can hardly accomplish a day of fasting for the purpose of prayer.

When I first examined His statement, I instinctively rejected the idea and needed a lot of persuasion to continue to explore it to discover that it is not a paradox. Rather, it is a universal spiritual and moral truth for all those who will receive and believe it. The picture that Jesus paints in this beatitude is a vivid one to those suffering through a famine as well as those who fear being without food and drink. But the Great Teacher was not addressing the issue of physical appetite and its need for satisfaction. He was speaking of an insatiable yearning for spirituality and chose words that all men and women, both then and now, may hear in plain, everyday speech and understand.

All of us, at one time or another, have experienced the pangs of hunger and thirst. Thus Jesus creates in our imagination the image of someone ravenous with hunger and parched with thirst, then tells us that when we long for righteousness just as a person does for food and water, we will join the happy of the Lord.

It is certainly not a pleasant picture if one should reflect a moment on the photographs of swollen-bellied babies from Sudan and other famine-ridden nations on our planet. Is this how we must crave for righteousness before we will be filled? Yes, if need be, for the happiness of being filled is granted only to those who, by faith, starve self and yearn after righteousness. Jesus' portrayal of a ravenous appetite mocks our self-complacency and destroys our self-satisfied brands of religion in which few ever come to really know that consuming anxiety for righteousness that Jesus stressed in this beatitude.

If we examine our hearts to compare and contrast our own languid and occasional impulses after godliness with the eagerness and intensity of our lust for material acquisition, entertainment, wealth, and success in life, we cannot help being astonished. The broad pathway of our desire runs earthward while only a tiny, narrow, almost obliterated track climbs the steep ascent toward heaven. Consequently, our unsatisfied longings lead to restlessness and disappointment because we fix our gaze on things that perish, things that can never satisfy our true human needs.

Jesus gave His sermon on the mount to a people who were poor and hungry as they suffered under the oppression of the arrogant rich. They also lived in a land in which the average annual rainfall wasn't more than 26 inches. Like much of southern California, Palestine, the Land of Promise, bordered on a large desert area. There even the most inhabited regions were dry, as we see illustrated by the story of Hagar and Ishmael in Genesis 21. Travelers who lost their way or missed the few springs along the route could easily die from thirst and hunger.

In addition to such physical aridity, many in the multitude listening to Jesus lacked imagination—were dull, lethargic, with small dreams and no vision of success in life. Undoubtedly, by the time Jesus spoke these words in Matthew 5:6, this crowd, having come from as far away as the Decapolis and perhaps even Syria, were hungry and unhappy. They not only experienced thirst under the increasingly hot sun, but were by then starving for food. Many stomachs must have growled from hunger while some even muttered openly of their desire for food and drink.

Jesus noticed their need, both physical and spiritual. Again, using a familiar human experience, He brought home truths of the kingdom when He declared, "Happy [are] those hungering and thirsting [not merely for food and drink, but] for righteousness," for "they shall be [satisfied]." He used the elemental human needs of hunger and thirst as spiritual metaphors and to reawaken hope and vision in their lives.

The thought that He wants us to cast aside our abundant material existence for starvation startles us. But in the light of this beatitude it seems that this is exactly what we must do. For it is a statistical fact that God's promptings are less likely to be responded to by people in prosperous nations than by those who are poor. The deep restless wants of our soul for things, the ambition so familiar to the human heart, must be exchanged for this supreme, divine gift.

Let us, then, take some time to examine this beatitude to find the blessings hidden in it. Perhaps we should first look at the word "righteousness." When I researched it in a variety of commentaries, I found myself astounded by the needless quibbling and theological debates over the word's precise meaning and importance. Here we will not add much more to the already-massive material on it except to point out that the Greek word for righteousness is *dikaiosune,* which comes from a word describing the exercise of a person's rights according to custom and culture.

Among the Greeks, whose Hellenistic culture had tremendous influence on the Jews in the time of Jesus, righteousness consisted in conformity to accepted customs, whether moral or not. For example, pederasty, an accepted form of homosexuality perpetrated by adult males on young boys, was a custom among educated elite Greeks. Back then, if you were an influential aging Greek male, society expected you to have at least one boy with whom you were sexually intimate (with the consent of approving parents). The Greeks used many different types of persuasion, including religion and literature, to convince their nation that it was an acceptable behavior. Some of the greatest love poems out of that era were written to little boys who were the victims of pederasty. As soon as these boys showed signs of adulthood, they found themselves rejected and replaced by younger ones. Only one young man, named Sporos, may have evaded such a fate. He was so feminine and attractive that emperors killed for him and poets swooned in sonnets about him.

Such pernicious activities even seeped into the Christian church at Rome and became so influential that the apostle Paul denounced the practice (Rom. 1:18-32). Today we find a similar attempt to make American society accept homosexuality. A variety of programs on prime-time television are being used to desensitize viewers into accepting this lifestyle as normal. They vociferously label as "right-wing religious nuts" those who oppose it. Thus today, as among the Greeks centuries ago, society determines righteousness, not by what God has instructed, but by the customs and culture of the day.

In the English language "righteousness" means to act rightly, uprightly, or wisely, and is summarized as right doing and being. Although it is the first thing that humans failed at, many Old Testament passages present righteousness as synonymous with salvation and denote it as a spiritual blessing (see Isa. 45:8; 46:12, 13; 51:5; 56:1; 59:17; 61:10). In almost every instance in which the word appears in the New Testament (nearly 100 times) righteousness connotes the right determined by the kingdom of heaven and not the predominant custom or culture of the day.

The Jews in Christ's time saw righteousness as essentially a matter of conformity to the requirements of the law as interpreted by their tradition. By the time Jesus used this word it had come to mean the character or quality of being right or just. The apostle Paul passionately emphasized that we cannot make ourselves righteous by keeping the law but can become righteous only by faith in Jesus Christ (Gal. 2:15-21).

The righteousness concept had a much broader and more profound meaning to Jesus than to the Greeks or Jews. To Him, it was the sum of all Christian graces and equivalent to holiness—personal, spiritual holiness of heart, body, and mind. The work of righteousness is peace and the assurance of His presence. Thus He called upon His followers to submit themselves to the righteousness of God instead of to the righteousness of their own culture or a strict adherence to the law (see Rom. 10:3 and Phil. 3:9).

Jesus was saying that according to the custom of heaven and the culture of the kingdom of grace, those who passionately desire His righteousness will be filled. He later declared that believers must "seek first the kingdom of God and His righteousness, and all these things shall be added to you" (Matt. 6:33, NKJV). To seek after—to yearn for—righteousness is to hunger and thirst after salvation.

To Christians, the righteousness of Christ is more than outwardly good conduct and conformity to moral laws and customs. It is God's own undeviating rightness, unfaltering love, and unfailing practice in the moral projection of the heavenly kingdom on earth. To hunger and thirst for God's righteousness is no extravagant ideal, but is the foundation of a healthy believer's life. The aching for righteousness is not the fear of punishment, but a longing after a clean heart like that expressed by David (Ps. 51). It is a relentless pursuit of God that creates an even more insatiable appetite for His presence the very moment we think we have found and caught up with Him.

Righteousness is a gift from God that He both imputes and imparts to us. It is imputed in that it brings justification, a legal term wherein a guilty sinner is made just by the blood of Jesus Christ. Those who surrender to God through repentance (Rom. 5:6-9) receive it immediately. And it is imparted because it provides sanctification, that daily transformation of a sinner through the empowering presence of the Holy Spirit and the indwelling Christ that enables us to conform to the divine character. The Christian must hunger and thirst for both aspects. As in physical hunger and thirst we experience intense craving, so also in spiritual hunger and thirst we should have sharp soul-pangs for the Lord our righteousness.

Jesus discussed the idea of spiritual thirst more fully some months after the Sermon on the Mount (John 4:7-30). In the story popularly referred to as "the woman at the well" He addressed the human need for fulfillment. As He and His disciples walked through the territory of Samaria they happened on a well. In reporting it, John emphasized the fact that Jesus *"had to pass through Samaria"* (verse 4) at a time when no normal Jew willingly traveled through that region, even though it was the most direct route between Jerusalem and Galilee.

Since open hostility existed between the Jews and Samaritans (similar to the conflict between Jews and Palestinians today), it was more prudent for Jews to take the long circuitous route than risk their lives on that shortcut. But Jesus, leaving in the early hours of the dawn, ignored the risks because *He had to* take this route with His disciples to keep a divine appointment with a desperately hungry and thirsty woman.

Every time I reflect on this story I find myself deeply moved by Jesus' thoughtfulness toward women. As a pastor who happens to be female, I function in a profession that imposes many restrictions on women, even though they may be called by God and endowed by His grace to be His messengers. Yet we are God's instruments fulfilling His prophecy of the last days (see Joel 2:28; also quoted in Acts 2:17, 18).

In addition, I operate under my own self-criticism, for none can be harder on us professional women than we are on ourselves. Furthermore, the church and the world often place many unrealistic and unattainable expectations on us. All these things contribute to feelings of insecurity. So when I read how Jesus went out of His way to touch that nameless woman's soul, I weep with gratitude for His grace, especially His tenderness toward women—including me!

When the sun had reached its zenith Jesus became dehydrated, weary, and hungry. Being fully human, as He was also fully God, Jesus experienced the common human need for food, water, and rest. So He sent His disciples for food, although I can't help thinking it was a ploy to temporarily get rid of them! He knew that the woman would not approach the well with so many Jewish men loitering around it. Then He sat on the curbstone of the well and waited for His appointment with destiny. He was extremely hungry, not for food, but for the soul of a sinner (John 4:34). Soon there came a woman, someone also intensely thirsty for that which only God could provide.

A well in those days was important not just for water but also as a meeting place between women who came to water their flocks and men who sought a marriage partner. It was the social place for singles, where virgins would appear in the cool of morning to draw water for their father's flocks or households, often with the hidden agenda of meeting the man of their dreams. Women who came to the wells in the heat of the day, however, did so because they wished to avoid gossip or shunning by others. Prostitutes also came to ply their trade at noon.

Abraham's servant went to a well to find a bride for Isaac (Gen. 24:11-18). Elsewhere Moses rescued a group of young maidens at noontime being driven away by shepherds who perhaps thought they were women of ill repute (Ex. 2:15-22). (Note that one of them later became Moses' wife.)

So there was Jesus, a single man, sitting at a well in a society that considered the well a place to meet marriageable girls and pick up wild women. At high noon a foreigner, a divorced woman with a bad reputation, came along. As she approached, Jesus did not flee from her polluting presence as any good rabbi would have. Instead He relaxed and initiated a conversation that might have seemed like a solicitation or proposition when He said, "Give Me a drink."

Her response bore this out when she said, "How is it that You, being a Jew, ask me for a drink since I'm a Samaritan woman?" (John 4:9). Basically she was saying, "Why are You, a Jew, coming on to me, a Samaritan?" And instead of rebuking her for her rudeness to Him (whom she may have perceived to be the rabbi Jim Bakker or Jimmy Swaggart of her time), plus her presumptuous thinking that He would cross their ethnic divide even for a secret, intimate liaison, Jesus seemed to play along with her.

"If you knew the gift of God, and who it is who says to you, 'Give Me a drink,'" He said, "you would have asked Him, and He would have given you living water" (verse 10). Now He had her full attention, for even though she could not articulate it, living water was what she desperately desired. He had touched the very core of her soul's hunger and thirst for fulfillment. The crux of what He was conveying was that "everyone who drinks of this water [pointing to the well on which He sat] will thirst again." However, "whoever drinks of the water that I [perhaps pressing an open palm against His chest] will give . . . shall never thirst; but the water that I will give . . . will become in [him or her] a well of water springing up to eternal life" (verses 13, 14).

After testing Him and engaging Him in a little theological bantering to make sure that He was who she was beginning to hope He was—one sent from God to save her—she was ready to hear and embrace this profound promise.

When we are hungry and thirsty for love, forgiveness, and acceptance, there's only One who can satisfy us: Jesus Christ, in an ongoing, personal relationship with Him. This nameless woman truly represents all who are seeking their purpose in life with a deep, insatiable hunger and thirst. The presence of God immediately filled her, instantly quenching her thirst. She "left her waterpot, and went into the city and said to the men, 'Come, see a man who told me all the things that I have done; this is not the Christ, is it?'" (verses 28, 29).

Jesus also spoke about the other word, "hunger" (John 6). After He miraculously fed 5,000 men and a multitude of women and children with five loaves and two fish, the people were astonished. "Therefore when the people saw the sign which He had performed, they said, 'This is truly the Prophet who is to come into the world'" (John 6:14; see also Deut. 18:15, 18).

On that occasion He perceived that the multitudes, perhaps instigated by Judas, "were intending to come and take Him by force to make Him king" (John 6:15). In fact, they pursued Him relentlessly. So He firmly and forcefully told them, "Truly, truly, I say unto you, you seek Me, not because you saw signs, but because you ate of the loaves, and were filled. Do not work for the food which perishes, but for the food which endures to eternal life, which the Son of Man will give to you, for on Him the Father, even God, has set His seal" (verses 26, 27).

Jesus was saying that indeed they were hungry, and yes, He had the ability to miraculously provide food for their physical nourishment, but that they shouldn't seek Him only because He took care of their natural needs. The same holds true for us today. The hunger for satisfaction, which we often interpret as a need for material contentment, is usually a spiritual one that only Jesus can satisfy. Their response, as is often ours today, was to ask for a sign that would prove that He really was the Messiah, the one who would bring bread from heaven as had Moses (verses 30, 31).

Their minds were so darkened by their lack of spiritual discernment that they couldn't understand the meaning of what Jesus said. Thus He retorted, "Truly, truly, I say to you, it is not Moses who has given you bread out of heaven, but it is My Father who gives you the true bread out of heaven. For the bread of God is that which comes down out of heaven, and gives life to the world" (verses 32, 33).

When their unspiritual minds still could not grasp these profound spiritual truths and they kept on asking Him to give them physical bread forever, He spoke plainly and said, *"I am the bread of life;* he who comes to Me will not hunger, and he who believes in Me will never thirst" (verse 35). Here is the answer to our hunger and thirst for satisfaction—Jesus Christ and none other. He is the only one who can fulfill our longing for peace and happiness.

As in previous beatitudes, this one also describes a dual experience. First, we observe the initial hunger and thirst that begins in the unconverted heart as the Holy Spirit prompts it to recognize its emptiness without Christ and to seek His gift of salvation. But after the sinner is saved, that hunger and thirst, though partially satisfied by the presence of the Savior, now grows into an insatiable desire for more.

The one who longs for the Savior and finds Him must, after conversion, yearn daily to be more like Him. The psalmist described this sensation as the panting of a renewed heart after God (see Ps. 42:1). One contemporary Christian author, Tommy Tenney, said the one who has such an experience becomes a "God chaser."

Remember when we were first converted, how we dreamed of capturing the world for Jesus? How we sought every opportunity to witness? Nothing could keep us away from prayer meetings and worship opportunities. We read every Christian book, bought every version of the Bible, and were willing to hurl ourselves against the walls of religious indifference to accomplish anything for our Lord.

Remember how obnoxious we seemed to others in our zeal to witness for the Lord? Well, I can't forget how annoying I was. My sister can't either, even though today we can look back and laugh at the times I turned off her television, without asking her permission, while she was watching her favorite program. Or the time I threw out her favorite meats because I thought they were unclean, shouting over her protests that "God said it and I believe it and that's enough for me!" Or the ways in which I corrected her when she tried to quote Scripture from *The Living Bible* by insisting that the only inspired word was the King James Version.

I was determined to win my entire family for God with vinegar that made their lives miserable and my testimony sour. But I thought I was simply sharing the joy of salvation. It is true that in any area of life a little learning is a dangerous thing, but especially so when it comes to religious ideas and practice. Thank God, He has since taught me that the sweet honey of grace is much more palatable and restorative than any strong dose of the bitter medicine of so-called truth.

What has happened since then to blunt the edge of our desire? How can we forget when once we hungered and thirsted after righteousness and cried out, "Give me souls or give me death"?

The time has come to stop being (if we have), and not go there (if we haven't yet become), so lackadaisical that we lose the sense of the warmth of our first love in those earlier days. Jesus said, Happy "are those who hunger and thirst for righteousness, for they shall be filled" (NKJV)—not in the future, but right now.

As you may have already noticed, I love to study the words God chose to convey His lessons. When I looked at the word "filled" in this beatitude, I became quite intrigued by the original meaning: to feed or fatten cattle, from the word for fodder or green grass. So let us put the promise that happy "are those who hunger and thirst for righteousness, for they shall be *filled*" into perspective.

Jesus deliberately said that they would be as the fatted calves, like those belonging to the wealthy that many of the poor, hungry multitudes had to tend daily. When God creates a hunger and thirst for salvation in a sinner, He fills also and fattens them, like those calves, to satisfaction.

In the words "they shall be filled" we have both the reason for happiness and a description of it. It consists of getting what we need from God, the most generous giver of every good and perfect gift (James 1:17). None of the pursuits and pleasures of this world or the pledges and promises of the devil can really outdo His giving or ever satisfy our human nature. When we dip our empty cups of hope in His well that never fails, God always fills them up with "a good measure—pressed down, shaken together, and running over" (Luke 6:38). Those who set their hearts and ambitions on the righteousness of Christ will find the thirst-quenching, hunger-filling satisfaction that paradoxically keeps us always wanting more even as we are happy and filled.

Once a real craving for God awakens in us, nothing short of a personal relationship with Him can daily satisfy our growing demand for more of Jesus. He leads us to new and more sincere desires every day by showing that He loves us in spite of all that we do and are. When we seem to present our worst side to the world and defame His Holy name—when we make a lie of the truth and present Him as a deadbeat dad who neglects His children—He does not reject us, as we deserve. Instead He sees the best—His Son—in us. In those times He cries out to the accusing principalities and powers, "This one is mine, [she or he] ravishes my heart!" (S. of Sol. 4:9).

Those who keep on hungering and thirsting after righteousness will find a satisfaction that drives them to want still more. It is like taking a breath after a deep dive in a swimming pool, only to realize that while one breath satisfies, it is not enough. You have to continue breathing, every gasp of air quickly leading to another.

Hope may be deferred for a long time. Believers may experience untold disappointments. But in the end they will not be put to shame. *They will be filled.* Like the prodigal son who realized his own hunger and thirst and went back to his father's house, so every sinner must return by faith to Christ in order to be satisfied.

Those who hunger and thirst after the righteousness of God will be filled with peace and happiness that no sorrow or pain can take away. They will exult with praise and thanksgiving and will be as the man in the story about a king's search for satisfaction and contentment.

The king was suffering from an extremely painful ailment when his physician told him that his only hope for a cure was to find a contented man, get his shirt, and wear it night and day. So the ruler quickly dispatched messengers throughout his realm in search of such an individual, with orders to bring back his shirt.

Months passed, and after a thorough search of the country, the messengers returned, but without the shirt. "Did you not find a contented man in all of my realm?" the king asked.

"Yes, O king" they replied. "We found one—just one in all your realm."

"Then why did you not bring back his shirt?" the king demanded.

"Master," his servants answered, now worried about their lives as they reluctantly gave the final answer. "The man had no shirt!"

Happy are those who have no shirt, but are contented knowing that their nakedness is covered by the rich robe of Christ's righteousness (Rev. 3:18).

Are you one of those who "can't get no satisfaction"? Then get rid of that old shirt and treasure nothing more than a hunger and thirst for Christ's righteousness, and you will be satisfied. George Knight mentioned in his commentary on Matthew that "as A. D. Martyn Lloyd-Jones puts it, hungering and thirsting after righteousness 'means that one's supreme desire in life is to know God and to be in fellowship with Him, to walk with God the Father, the Son, and the Holy Spirit' " (*The Abundant Life Bible Amplifier—Matthew,* p. 86). Wow! This means we get all three in one. No wonder Jesus said we would be filled!

Then, like Paul, we will not complain about that which we lack or lose. Instead, we will learn to be content in whatever circumstances we find ourselves in life (see Phil. 4:11-13). God also promises the following to all who are in Christ:

You "will hunger no more, nor thirst anymore, nor will the sun beat down on [you], nor any heat; for the Lamb in the center of the throne will be [your] shepherd, and will guide [you] to springs of the water of life; and God shall wipe away every tear from [your] eyes" (Rev. 7:16, 17).

Do you hunger and thirst after righteousness but feel that you are not worthy to receive these promises? Are you worried that you cannot afford them? Listen to this: "Ho! Every one who thirsts, come to the waters; and you who have no money come, buy and eat. Come, buy wine and milk without money and without cost" (Isa. 55:1).

O happy day! So, come, Lord Jesus. Come fill us now, O Son of righteousness, so that we may be genuinely happy and satisfied even as our hunger and thirst for You intensifies.

CHAPTER

A Ministry to the Miserable

Happy "are the merciful, for they shall receive mercy."
Matthew 5:7.

Before he passed away, Julian Legrand, a great and wealthy Paris merchant of the past century, reported the following event in his own life. He said that the business firm he had established had fallen into serious financial straits. After extensive examination of the company's operation, he discovered that it would take more than $100,000 to save it—an enormous sum in those days, equivalent to at least $1 million today.

Although he exhausted every avenue for loans, no one would lend him a dollar. One day, after being rejected by banks and business associates more often than he cared to remember, he returned to his office, dejected and in despair. While sitting there, he heard a soft knock on his door. The man who entered came to his desk, exhibited a warm smile and most pleasant demeanor, and said, "Mr. Legrand, the word is out in the business community that you are in need of money."

"Yes," replied the merchant, humbled and embarrassed by these circumstances, "we certainly are in a desperate situation."

"How much do you need?" the stranger asked kindly.

"Not less than $100,000," replied Legrand, who decided to humor the man to see where he was going with his questions.

"Draw me your note, and let's make a contract for the amount you need, without interest for one year, and I will give you a check for it," the man continued in a more serious tone. He then placed on Legrand's desk evidence of his ability to back his words with the necessary resources.

When Legrand expressed surprise at his generosity, the stranger explained, "When I was a little boy attending public school, you came there as one of the commissioners on examination day. I was poor and shabbily dressed and thought that you would of course pay attention only to the rich children. I expected no recognition for myself.

"That day I recited poorly, but after the exercises you put your hand on my head and spoke some kind words to me. Urging me to persevere and telling me that I could do better if I tried, you assured me that the way to honor was an open door to all alike. On that memorable day you said that all I had to do was to be resolute and push on.

"That, sir, was the turning point in my life. From that hour my soul has aspired for greater things, and I have never accomplished anything without blessing you in my heart. I have prospered and am very wealthy. I now offer you but a poor return for the soul-wealth you gave me in that bygone time" (adapted from Paul Lee Tan, *Encyclopedia of 15,000 Illustrations,* p. 1485).

The moral of this story is that a good deed does not often go unnoticed or unrewarded. It also confirms the words of our Lord that happy "are the merciful, for they shall receive mercy." However, since learning the true meaning of mercy, I have become somewhat frustrated with many of these touching testimonies about rich rewards reaped from unintentional acts of kindness.

Such accounts tend to foster a dysfunctional spirituality that expects a grand return on the investment of kindness (purpose-driven or otherwise), especially if done to the poor and indigent around us. As a result, many practitioners of the Christian faith have come to believe that if they give food or old, unwanted clothing to the needy, or put in a little time in feeding the homeless, they are "merciful" and will eventually reap great rewards.

It reminds me of an experience with my son when he was about 3 years old. He was just about the cutest little boy one could ever come across. I do not say this just because he is my son, but because almost everyone in Hartford, Connecticut, where we lived, would comment on his charismatic character when they saw him. Back then strangers seemed kinder and gentler, and there was not such a threat of his being kidnapped and abused. Oftentimes people would give him a piece of candy as they remarked on his attractiveness. One day we entered a department store just as a man was leaving. He bent down, greeted my son, and said, "You are such a cute little guy!" Then after smiling and tweeking my son's cheek, he began to walk away. Instantly my son yelled out, to my utter embarrassment, "So where's my candy?" Like some believers today, he had come to expect that a reward accompanied every compliment.

We have done little to educate Christians into a proper understanding of the biblical meaning of "mercy." Usually we restrict it to kindness to the poor or mere humanitarianism and pity. But in the Bible, especially as used by Jesus in this beatitude, mercy comes from the term *eleemon,* from which our English word "eleemosynary"—"relating to and supported by charity or devoted to alms"—derives. The Hebrew equivalent, *chesedh,* underscores a blessing of extra goodness and an act of divine favor demonstrated by kindness and graciousness to a known enemy (cf. Rom. 5:6-10). A merciful person was characterized not simply as one who possessed pity, but as one actively compassionate and forbearing with an offender or subject, as God is with us.

It is worthy to note also that "compassionate" comes from the Greek word that describes the inward parts of the human body, such as heart, liver, lungs, and kidneys. The ancients considered the organs to be the seat of human passion and the center of personal feelings and sensibility affected by pain and suffering, especially that of others. It means that mercy is not just a shallow attempt to win favor with God, but a deep inner sentiment that responds with strong sorrow for those struck by misfortune.

When speaking of mercy, William Barclay said:

"It does not mean only to sympathize with a person in the popular sense of the term; it does not mean simply to feel sorry for someone in trouble. *Chesedh, mercy,* means the ability to get right inside the other person's skin. . . . Clearly this is much more than an emotional wave of pity; clearly this demands a quite deliberate effort of the mind and of the will" (*The Gospel of Matthew,* vol. 1, p. 98).

That was exactly what Jesus did. He got into our skin by becoming a human being (Phil. 2:7) so that He could save us. He was "made like His brethren in all things, so that He might become a merciful and faithful high priest in things pertaining to God, to make propitiation for the sins of the people" (Heb. 2:17). Becoming human made it possible for Jesus to see life through our eyes, to feel the sting of pain and the hurt of betrayal, to identify with our anguish and anger. "For since He himself was tempted in that which He has suffered, He is able to come to the aid of those who are tempted" (verse 18), observed the author of the book of Hebrews. Furthermore, He can sympathize with our weaknesses. He understands our misery because He is "one who has been tempted in all things as we are, yet without sin" (Heb. 4:15).

Until we can show a generous spirit and treat with kindness those who will dip their hand in the bowl with us and then betray us (as Judas did Jesus [Matt. 26:23, 47-53]), we have not been merciful. Jesus Himself said:

"You have heard that it was said, *'you shall love your neighbor and hate your enemy,' but I say to you, love your enemies* and pray for those who persecute you, so that you may be sons of your Father who is in heaven; for He causes His sun to rise on the evil and the good, and sends rain on the righteous and the unrighteous. *For if you love those who love you, what reward do you have?"* (Matt. 5:43-46).

Just as breathing is necessary for our survival, so are acts of kindness normal behavior in the life of a believer. That's why there is no reward for those actions. They are simply things we ought to do as imitators of Christ and as sons and daughters of God.

Being kind to a known enemy is a most difficult proposition. That's the reason God gave the virtue of mercy as a spiritual gift (Rom. 12:8). It cannot be learned or earned and must be its own reward. To put it simply, mercy is spiritual "Red Cross" aid to God's enemies. No matter what their condition, they need the divine mercy demonstrated in the acts of His faithful followers.

During the time of Jesus many religious leaders lost sight of this interpretation of mercy. Arrogant and abusive to those lacking material possessions, they punished the poor for the smallest infraction, even if they themselves were blatantly guilty of the same deeds. A story that demonstrates the socioeconomic disparity between rich and poor and their treatment of them was the parable of the wicked steward (Matt. 18:23-34). Jesus used it to remind Peter of the divine concept of forgiveness and grace that does not bear a grudge, keep score of offenses, or remember past injuries. It also underscored the fact that all have sinned and, from the divine perspective, are insolvent debtors. If God should deal with men and women in strict justice as the rich religious leaders did with the poor, all would be condemned.

Jesus also used another popular local tale about the rich man and Lazarus (Luke 16:20-30) to demonstrate the great gulf between the wealthy and beggars of His day. He was emphasizing the inhumane attitudes toward the indigent demonstrated by a group of religious leaders who had seized the occasion to scoff at Jesus' teachings. Notice how severely He denounced them before revealing their conceit via the parable. "You are those who justify yourselves in the sight of men, but God knows your hearts; for that which is highly esteemed among men is detestable in the sight of God" (verse 15).

Unfortunately, some Christians have taken the story of the rich man and Lazarus out of context and therefore miss the point. They use it to engage in theological debates about Jesus' opinion on the state of the dead. But He was simply showing those hard-hearted religionists the significance of unconditional mercy to the humble and needy.

Jesus practiced what He preached. He repeatedly extended grace and mercy to the scribes, Pharisees, Sadducees, and Herodians, all of whom made it their business to entrap Him and kill Him (see Mark 12:13-40). He also showed mercy to even the merciless, such as Simon the leper (Luke 7:36-50).

Biblical mercy is never harsh, cruel, oppressive, or injurious in any way. Operating from empathy (not sympathy, its negative counterpart), it is the positive response to the needs of others. It evokes compassion for those caught in the web of sin—compassion so intense that people will risk their safety and forgo personal ease, interest, or gratification to bring relief to those in need.

At the height of the terrorist atrocities a few years ago, two young women missionaries found themselves captives in Afghanistan. They had risked their lives to bring the good news of God's grace to the oppressed people, especially women, of that region. After their rescue they personified the mercy Jesus spoke of in His fifth beatitude when they declared that if the opportunity ever came, they would again return to share the gospel.

Are you involved in a ministry? Do you practice being merciful to the miserable in mind, soul, and spirit? Or are you doing it to be noticed? Remember that Jesus warned us about the latter when He said: "Beware of practicing your righteousness before men to be noticed by them; otherwise you have no reward with your Father who is in heaven. So when you give to the poor, do not sound a trumpet before you, as the hypocrites do in the synagogues and in the streets, so that they may be honored by men. Truly I say to you, they have their reward in full" (Matt. 6:1, 2).

Mercy is a holy disposition of the spirit, an inward quality that enables one to weep with those who weep (Rom. 12:15). It tempers justice. In fact, when "mercy and truth are met together," "righteousness and peace have kissed each other" (Ps. 85:10, KJV). True mercy refuses to take revenge, even if one has the right to do so. Nor is it the foolish sentimentality that flouts the requirements of justice so pervasive in our society today. That kind of mercy inclines many not only to sympathize with those who deserve punishment for their heinous crimes, but to use our legal system to get them off as long as the price is right.

Some time ago I watched a documentary on justice in America. The narrator focused on a serial killer, referred to by the media as the night stalker, who had terrorized southeastern Californians for almost 18 months during the 1980s, killing 14 people and permanently disabling several others. One juror told the interviewer that she was so moved by "mercy" for this man that despite the fact that he taunted the court with his satanic signs and gestures throughout the trial, she wanted to vote to acquit him. Even before he had his turn to speak, the accused killer disrupted the court with gross details as to how he murdered his victims and the manner in which they begged for mercy before they died. The juror said she wanted to help him and almost compromised the case by baking him cookies during the trial. Afterward she dedicated her life to finding ways to free him from death row, even though he had never shown any sign of remorse or the remotest sense of repentance. She claimed to be doing all this in the name of mercy.

Anything that attempts to cancel or modify a justly deserved punishment, especially of an unrepentant person, is not holy, but is ungodly and even satanic. Even though God forgives the repentant perpetrator, they must face the consequences of their actions. Those who reject His forgiveness may prosper in this life, but in the end they will face the second death, i.e., everlasting separation from God and permanent destruction in the lake of fire (Rev. 20:11-15).

I am not endorsing the warped concept of a God who can't wait to wipe out sinners. God is patient with us far beyond my understanding or human appreciation. The Bible, however, clearly states that at the end of time God will do a strange thing—an unusual act—by requiring those whose names are "not found written in the book of life [to be] thrown into the lake of fire" alongside Satan, for whom it was made in the first place (verse 15).

In the kingdom of God mercy never cancels the consequences of sin. It simply provides forgiveness for the repentant sinner and empowers those who receive it to face their punishment with Christ on their side. The difference between our attitude to mercy and Jesus' is that while we plot how to protect the community from being robbed and plan how to prevent its citizens from being hurt, He has also provided a way to save the person who does the injury! We study how to keep our material goods safe and secure while Jesus prepares a way to keep the thief from stealing—not by locks or prisons, but by being turned into an honest person through the ministry of mercy.

In Shakespeare's *Merchant of Venice,* when Shylock claims his rights according to the letter of the law, Portia pleads for mercy, saying: "Earthly power doth then show like God's when mercy seasons justice." Mercy that is "like God's" is not mere sentiment but the effort to redeem, to win the evildoer to all that she or he might be in Christ. Anyone who has attempted this knows that it requires a great sacrifice on the part of the merciful, just as it did on the part of Jesus to extend compassion to a world spinning out of control and rebelling against God (John 3:16-18).

There is no greater revenge than to minister to those who have betrayed or injured us, and have God turn them into saints so that they, thereafter, will have to live with us as brothers and sisters in the kingdom of God. I had such an experience several years ago. My hairdresser ineptly gave me a perm that had chemicals in it that were too strong for me. Not only did I have an extended bad-hair day, but also she managed to give me a third-degree burn on my scalp that took several months to heal with some quite expensive medication from a dermatologist. I also had to wear a wig to cover my embarrassment.

When I confronted her with the damage she had done, she tried to sully my reputation with some of her clients who were members of my church. Many people suggested that I should sue her. I could have done so because I had a good case against her, but I realized that the woman did not know the Lord. Her response had emerged from a heart of misery, and there is none more miserable than the unconverted. So under the prompting of the Holy Spirit, who encouraged me to be merciful, I determined that my best response was to win her to the Lord so that she would have to live with me in the kingdom of grace as my sister.

I began by restraining my desires to retaliate as I set out on a mission of mercy. She responded positively to my acts of forgiveness, demonstrated primarily by the fact that I continued to have her take care of my hair. I can't describe—and won't take the time to tell you— how I grimaced with fear each time she gave me a shampoo, but I gracefully deterred her from applying further perms.

Eventually she accepted invitations to attend my church and home Bible study group. In time she gave her life to the Lord, joined our community of faith, and left the hairdressing business, for which I am eternally grateful. Today my sister in Christ is one of the most merciful nurses in her profession.

The mercy in which God forgives us is not a legal arrangement, but is a gracious, seeking love that receives those who come as they are. The one condition is that when we find ourselves convicted by the Holy Spirit (John 16:8) we then repent and turn from evil's hard and loveless ways and step into the new world of grace in which love reigns supreme in everything.

God extends the spirit of unconditional love to both the just and the unjust (Matt. 5:45). Even those prodigals who have not yet returned to the Father's house also experience God's mercy (see Rom. 5:6). To the one who comes home, however, Jesus declares that there is a special gift of mercy for them (Matt. 5:7). They leave the life of the miserable behind and thereafter become and are known as happy.

Believers in God receive a beautiful and encouraging exhortation to "draw near with confidence to the throne of grace, so that we may receive mercy and find grace to help in time of need" (Heb. 4:16). The first and last great effect of God's throne of grace is mercy.

The experience that brings us within the glory of divine mercy may occur in two ways. The first results from the very effort to overcome our bitterness when wronged. Those who have done this know that it is not an easy task. It lays a cross of godly sorrow on our heart as we sense the pain Christ endured to save us. We also feel the mocking and rejection of the guilty (see Matt. 27:39-45). This very experience, however, is the fountainhead of happiness for the merciful. Only they have some grasp of what it meant for Jesus to suffer for our sin, so that Scripture could say of Him that "for the joy set before Him [He] endured the cross" (Heb. 12:2). And they understand what it cost Jesus to pray for mercy for His foes.

Second, our vision of God in Christ—suffering, forgiving, and redeeming—engraves a sense of our own unworthiness on our souls and awakens a tremendous gratitude that our neighbor's wrongs seem as small, easily overcome barriers. No one on earth or among the fallen angels can ever harm us in the way that sinners have hurt Jesus. Thus we cannot and will not find our place in God's mercy until we show it toward others, no matter how hurtful their words, acts, or deeds may be. Mercy must become the very habit of our life—like breathing—as we mature in Christ.

But mercy is never afraid to exercise what many refer to as tough love. We see this illustrated in an Old Testament story about Saul, the first king of Israel. One day the newly anointed king received divine instructions to kill the enemy, Agag, and utterly destroy all the Canaanite ruler's people. But after Saul deliberated with his leaders, he decided to ignore God's decision and exercise his version of mercy by sparing the enemy. When Samuel, the prophet of God who delivered that message to Saul, saw that the king had disobeyed the Lord, he became very distressed. Saul explained that he did not consider that the Lord had really sent him on a mission to "utterly destroy the sinners, the Amalekites, and fight against them until they are exterminated" (1 Sam. 15:18), so he did not obey the divine directive. Israel's first king could not see that Agag's and the Amalekites' cup of sin had overflowed as they refused to repent. Neither did he understand that God was using him to execute divine judgment upon them. In the end, it was Samuel himself who took the sword and executed Agag that day (verses 18-33). Was Saul being merciful and Samuel a cruel fanatic?

Time eventually demonstrated that Saul was more interested in building a monument for himself throughout his reign than obeying God (verses 12, 22, 23). When confronted by Samuel, the king said the right things and showed remorse—but not repentance, for his heart was far from his words. He tried to blame his actions on public pressure (verses 24, 25, 30). Saul also attempted to excuse himself by insisting that the reason he did not destroy the Amalekite booty and captured livestock was that he wanted to sacrifice the animals to God. His disobedience caused Saul to lose the prize he treasured most—the kingdom of Israel (verses 23-29). It earned him some of the harshest words God has ever spoken to His people when Samuel said, "Has the Lord as much delight in burnt offerings and sacrifices as in obeying the voice of the Lord? Behold, to obey is better than sacrifice, and to heed than the fat of rams. For rebellion is as the sin of divination, and insubordination is as iniquity and idolatry" (verses 22, 23).

Those who refuse to repent and return to a saving relationship with God—those who seek to destroy His people—He will in the end have to put to death. The apostle James noted that "judgment will be merciless to one who has shown no mercy" (James 2:13). It is not up to the believer to put nonbelievers to death. We should wait for the Lord's judgment. Until then, believers must be willing to risk life and limb to be merciful and share the gospel with wretched and pitiable sinners (such as we once were [Eph. 2:1-3]) so that they also may be saved.

The mercy that Jesus promises to those who are merciful is not an outgrowth of normal human nature. Yes, the world is full of philanthropic nonbelievers whose sympathy for the suffering and readiness to forgive those who have wronged them sometimes surpass and embarrass that of some believers. The God who promised in His Word that "mercy triumphs over judgment" (James 2:13) will not forget them. They have their reward, even in the present world.

All mercy results from the prompting of the Holy Spirit. But the mercy that Jesus promised would bring the greatest happiness originates in an intimate relationship with God. It never takes into consideration how often one has been wronged, but is willing to restrain bitterness and seek the betterment of others, even aggressors.

Abraham's merciful heart, even after his nephew had wronged him, led him to rescue Lot despite great risk (Gen. 14). Joseph, despite the fact that his brothers grievously mistreated him, still freely forgave them and took them into his heart and home (Gen. 45). Moses, even though his sister, Miriam, rebelled against his authority and the Lord struck her with leprosy, still pleaded with God to heal her (Num. 12). And it was mercy on the part of David that caused him to spare the life of Saul, his archenemy, when he caught the king asleep in a cave (1 Sam. 24).

The mercy we are talking about focuses especially on the spiritual condition of human beings, distinguishing it from the kindness of many benevolent organizations and philanthropies that pity and administer to the temporal needs of the poor but have no concern for their eternal prospects.

Everyone must carefully heed this beatitude. It is the duty of the preacher and teacher, the employer and employee, the rich and poor believer in Christ, to be merciful. And the attitude in which we extend such mercy is vital too. The apostle Paul declared: "Since we have gifts that differ according to the grace given to us, each of us is to exercise them accordingly: if prophecy, according to the proportion of his faith; . . . *he who shows mercy, with cheerfulness*" (Rom. 12:6-8).

Just as the emotionally disinterested or spiritually detached and physically distant people cannot exercise true mercy, so it cannot be shown out of dutiful resignation by believers. As God loves the cheerful giver, He equally treasures the ones who respond to the precept of mercy with a joyous spirit (2 Cor. 9:7).

There is nothing worse than those who act as though being in the mission field is a burden they have to endure. If that's the case, then that person shouldn't be there, for missionary work and mercy must reflect a cheerful heart. God said that the merciful are happy, for they themselves "shall receive mercy." One commentator said that "we could paraphrase this beatitude: 'O the bliss of one who identifies with and assists others in need—who gets inside their skin so completely he sees with their eyes and thinks with their thoughts and feels with their feelings. The one who does that will find that others do the same for him when he is in need' " (Charles Swindoll, *Improving Your Serve,* p. 113).

Some old-time theologians used to say that the mercy promised in this beatitude is not the reward of condignity, one that is wholly deserved, but of congruity, one that is harmonious with life. It does not confirm the legalistic idea of salvation by works or any other belief that by charity we can make ourselves satisfactory to God for our sins. Our acts of mercy are not meritorious in God's sight. If that were the case, Jesus would have said, "Happy are the merciful, for they shall obtain justice," because that which is meritorious is due reward by legal right. But when mercy results from a heart filled with His Spirit, it is grace done cheerfully that God rewards both in this life and the next.

This fifth beatitude has nothing to do with how one is to be saved. Rather it enunciates how God wants us to live during our life on earth. For instance, Jesus said, "If you forgive others for their transgressions, your heavenly Father will also forgive you. But if you do not forgive others, then your Father will not forgive your transgressions" (Matt. 6:14, 15).

He also said, "Do not judge so that you will not be judged. For in the way you judge, you will be judged; and by your standard of measure, it will be measured to you" (Matt. 7:1, 2). In other words, you will reap that which you sow (Gal. 6:7).

When I first became a Christian, I had a hard time with the way people gossiped about me. It seemed as though not a day passed without my hearing of someone who had said a slanderous thing or deliberately misinterpreted what I said. I couldn't understand why people would say such things about someone who was really trying hard to hold on to Jesus Christ and her newfound faith.

One day, as I was weeping and complaining to God, I cried out, "Why are these people hurting me so much, and why are You allowing them to do so?"

Instantly the Lord pointed out to me what was then one of the most shocking revelations of my life. He said to me quietly, "Daughter, as soon as you stop gossiping about others, they will stop gossiping about you."

The thought astonished me, but right then I determined not to gossip anymore. It took a lot of discipline, but believe me, within a week of my ceasing such behavior, I did not hear of a hurtful word being said about me. Perhaps people continued to gossip, but no one mentioned it to me. Later when a few did report some things, God took out the sting so that I no longer felt devastated by it.

About the same time that God alerted me to my strong propensity toward gossiping, I read that we should beware more of the person who repeats gossip than the one who originates it, perhaps in hurt and anger. Those who hear gossip and do not put a stop to it, or give it credence by their silence and then repeat it later, are more dangerous than those who actually start it. Anyone who perpetuates unchecked gossip is not a friend, but a mortal enemy. That also helped change my mind about quoting unproven statements or saying things about others that should be left unsaid.

Now I am at the place in my life where I am committed to live the truth, and any false statement or curses against me I believe will happen only as God allows them. I have learned a lot about my own shortcomings from those painful experiences and have matured in Christ through them. That is the reason I say, in the words of David, "Let them alone and let them curse, for the Lord has told them. Perhaps the Lord will look on my affliction and return good to me instead of their falsehoods and curses" (see 2 Sam. 16:11, 12).

Happy "are the merciful, for they shall receive [or obtain] mercy" is a principle that has proven itself true on many occasions. Relating those events would fill a vast library of volumes of personal testimonies. Try being merciful, in the biblical sense! Not only will you like the freedom from the heart-wrenching pain of being harmed; you will be happy as God piles mercies upon mercies into your own life.

We will receive three kinds of rewards. The first is an inward benefit. The one who shows mercy to others gains something. "A gracious woman attains honor. . . . The merciful man does himself good, but the cruel man does himself harm" (Prov. 11:16, 17). In fact, Jesus seemed to be echoing the statement "happy is he who is gracious to the poor" (Prov. 14:21) in His beatitude. He appeared to be simply repeating principles He had given to the ancient Israelites, principles still relevant as we journey toward our longed-for hope, His second coming.

Second, we obtain an outward reward. Forgiveness from God is not the only experience. Kindness at the hand of others is also a reward of mercy (Gal. 6:7). Since we prefer blessings and not curses and like to be treated well, we ought to sow kindness, mercy, justice, and goodness consistently. People's lives are definitely happier when others treat them well, so let us go out and blanket the world with mercy.

The third reward is both internal and external. The psalmist declared its dual aspects as he praised God for His deliverance (Ps. 18). James demonstrated the benefits when he said: "For judgment will be merciless to one who has shown no mercy; mercy triumphs over judgment" (James 2:13). If you fear the judgment, you can find assurance of escaping condemnation (John 5:24; Rom. 8:1) simply by being merciful (see also 2 Tim. 1:16-18).

When one of Jesus' brothers, who at first rejected Him and tried to thwart His ministry to the miserable people of his day, finally came to his senses, he left us the following legacy. He said: "Keep yourselves in the love of God, waiting anxiously for the mercy of our Lord Jesus Christ to eternal life" (Jude 21).

I know that the catalog of sins on my page in the book of life far outweighs any act of mercy that I may perform, but thank God for the mercy of Jesus Christ, whose blood has obliterated them.

God described Himself as merciful (Ex. 33:19; 34:6). How pleased He must be when we imitate His compassion, mercy, and love. When we exercise forgiveness to undeserving people, we catch a glimpse inside God's heart. In gratitude for His grand acts of mercy to me, I have determined to go and do likewise as I learn to heed prayerfully the exhortations to be devoted to one another in brotherly and sisterly love (Rom. 12:10 and Gal. 6:2). As "those who have been chosen of God, holy and beloved, put on a heart of compassion, kindness, humility, gentleness and patience, bearing with one another, and forgiving each other, whoever has a complaint against anyone; just as the Lord forgave you, so also should you. Beyond all these things put on love, which is the perfect bond of unity" (Col. 3:12-14).

A man built a large and prosperous business through the honest toil and unselfish cooperation of his fellow workers. As he grew older he became concerned about the future interest of his enterprise, because his only surviving relatives consisted of three nephews.

One day he called them into his office and said to them, "One of you will be my successor, but before I determine which one, I have a task for you to perform." He then handed each youth a coin with instructions to "go and buy something with this coin that will fill this room as full as possible. Spend no more than I gave you, and return at sunset."

All day long the young men scouted the marketplace. When the shadows of evening lengthened into dusk, they made their way back to their uncle, who was waiting in his office. The first nephew dragged a huge bale of straw into the room, which, after he had untied it, hid two walls of the office. It did not measure up, in spite of the compliments of the others as they helped to clear it away. The second young man brought in two bags of thistledown, which, when released, filled half the room. Again the others cheered, but the uncle was not yet impressed.

Finally, the third young man stepped forward, looking somewhat forlorn. "Uncle, I gave most of my coin to a hungry child, and some of what

I had left I gave to a church that I passed on the way here. Then, with my final penny, I bought a flint and this tiny candle, which I will light before I leave, for I have failed, as did my cousins." Striking the flint, he lit the candle, which in turn filled every corner of the room with its light. The old man blessed him and declared him his successor.

Happy are those who perform a ministry to the miserable, for they shall receive unexpected and abundant mercy from God.

CHAPTER

Hygiene for the Holy

Happy "are the pure in heart, for they shall see God."
Matthew 5:8.

A distinguished pastor had one of his members, a physician, approach him with concern about the minister's health. He handed the pastor some tickets and said, "Take these. You need to see this play." His pastor glanced at the tickets and, seeing that they were to the kind he could not conscientiously attend, returned them to the doctor and said kindly, "Thank you very much, but I can't take these tickets."

"Why not?" queried the physician.

"Doctor," the pastor replied, placing his hand in a friendly gesture on the doctor's shoulder, "it's this way. You're a physician—a surgeon, in fact. When you operate, you scrub your hands meticulously until you are especially clean. You wouldn't dare operate with dirty hands, right?" The doctor nodded in agreement. "As a servant of Christ," the minister continued, "I assist Him in radical surgery on human souls. I wouldn't dare do my service with a dirty heart."

Just as there is a process and expectation of cleanliness for surgeons, so also there's an inner hygiene for the servants of God who aspire to be holy as He is holy (Lev. 11:44, 45; cf. 1 Peter 1:15, 16). Jesus endorsed this when He announced, Happy "are the pure in heart." He was underscoring holiness as a code of Christian health care that, when practiced by believers, guarantees them the ability to accomplish two important ideals.

First, to be holy in all our behavior, as is the Holy One who called us so that we may "conduct [ourselves] in fear during the time of [our] stay on earth" (1 Peter 1:17). Second, to be able to attain that which the Bible said no one has ever done before, i.e., to see God and live (Ex. 33:20; cf. John 1:18; see Rev. 21:1-4).

One of the most beautiful poems penned by David is the anthem for the establishment of Jerusalem as the city of the great king. He wrote it after he captured the Jebusite stronghold of Zion (2 Sam. 5:6-10). As David moved the ark from its temporary resting place to the tent he had prepared for it in the city of Jerusalem, the people sang this song, chanting the words at the foot of the hill before the procession began to ascend the heights into the city. "Who may ascend into the hill of the Lord? And who may stand in His holy place? He who has clean hands and a pure heart, who has not lifted up his soul to falsehood and has not sworn deceitfully" (Ps. 24:3, 4).

Many commentators have suggested that this portion of the intricate poem is an expansion of the thought underlying Jesus' statement Happy "are the pure in heart, for they shall see God."

One of the most sacred stories in the Old Testament tells how Moses asked God to show him His glory. God replied, "You cannot see My face, for no man can see Me and live!" (Ex. 33:20). But because He loved Moses so much and did not want to refuse his request, the Lord set him in the cleft of a rock, partially covered him with His hand, and passed by so that Moses could see only His back (verse 23).

In this sixth beatitude Jesus removed the believer from the cleft of the rock as He revealed the constitution of the newly established kingdom of God on earth. Whereas Moses gazed only on the retreating procession of God, we are now called to look up and see Him face to face and live—on the condition that we are consistently nurturing a heart that is pure by grace.

An epigram states that no power on earth can neutralize the influence of a life motivated by a pure heart. In fact, a basic requirement for participation in God's kingdom is a divinely cleansed heart. Not only is God watching to bless us, and the enemy to curse us, but people around us are also keenly aware of our behavior and note when we make a lie of the truth (James 3:14).

It reminds me of a story about a well-known pastor who took a bus from his home in the suburbs to his church in the heart of his city. Although it was unusual for him to use public transportation, in an effort to mingle in the world familiar to many of his members he got on the bus, paid the driver, and sat down. As he counted the change the driver had given him, he realized that he had received too much.

His first thought was one of praise: "How wonderful is God's providence as He finds the most unusual ways to provide a little extra for His people!" But as he considered keeping the extra cash, his conscience convicted him that it was not a gift from God. The longer he waited to return the money, the more his conscience pricked him and the deeper the conviction that what he was thinking of doing was wrong. As he walked to the door of the bus to get off at his destination, his conscience made one final, strong appeal to return the money. Handing over the extra change, he quietly said to the driver, "When I got on the bus, you accidentally gave me too much."

"Pastor," the driver replied with a wry smile, "it was no accident at all. I attended your church yesterday and heard your sermon on honesty. I just thought I'd have a little fun and test you to see if you practice what you preach."

To understand further the significance of this pure-in-heart beatitude, it is important to note that the Sermon on the Mount has a unified structure. Martyn Lloyd-Jones discussed this aspect in his book *Studies in the Sermon on the Mount.* He suggested that the first three beatitudes—on being poor in spirit, on mourning, and on being meek—are more concerned with the outward, temporal human needs and our egocentric consciousness of them.

The fourth beatitude is the center of the nine because after the first part that highlights the human needs of hunger and thirst or search for satisfaction comes a powerful provision that reminds us that God truly takes care of everything. It promises satisfaction that causes one to feel filled like contented calves in green pastures rich with fodder or grass.

The next three beatitudes—calling for us to be merciful, pure in heart, and peacemakers—underscore the inner spiritual results, for that is exactly how those who are satisfied in Jesus behave. The last two beatitudes, which are often combined as one—being persecuted for righteousness' sake; being reviled, and spoken against falsely for His name's sake—are experiences along our spiritual journey after we have recognized our human needs, found satisfaction, and begun consistently to live a life in Christ.

A final illustration on this unity shows that the first beatitude (poor in spirit) corresponds with the fifth (the merciful). The merciful are those who realize that we are all poor and have nothing in ourselves. We need the grace of God to survive. Recognizing and admitting our poverty of spirit is a most essential first step in the process of reconciliation with God and others (2 Cor. 5:16-19). It is only after we have received God's grace that we are able to be kind to a known enemy. Also Scripture challenges us to do nothing from selfishness or empty conceit, but from true humility, treating others as being more important than ourselves (Phil. 2:3).

The second beatitude (those who mourn) corresponds with the sixth (the pure in heart), the one we are currently examining. Those who mourn do so because they realize the state of their heart, one pervaded by sin and separated from God. They sorrow not only because they did things that were wrong, but when we are born again, we experience a tremendous conflict, or war, between the old carnal nature and the new nature in Christ (Rom. 7:15-25). It is a terrible dilemma. The only way to receive God's gift of a pure heart is to realize that, because of sin, we all have impure hearts. Thus we must learn to surrender our hearts, with all we hold dear, so that we can see Him and live.

The third beatitude (about the meek) corresponds with the seventh (the peacemakers), which we will explore in the next chapter. Only those who are truly meek will be able to make peace and not war. In the first three beatitudes we went up one side of the mountain of need, according to Martyn Lloyd-Jones, and reached the summit in the fourth. We come down the other side of the mountain in the next three, then experience the joyous results of having climbed up that sacred mount in the last two beatitudes.

Some of the phrases Jesus used in the Beatitudes to describe these experiences came from the Psalms, but the originality lies in the fact that He put new value and meaning in them, making them prominent principles. For example, we hear echoes of the third beatitude in Psalm 37:9: "For evildoers will be cut off, but those who wait for the Lord, they will inherit the land [earth]." The beatitude we are now exploring, Happy "are the pure in heart, for they shall see God," comes from Psalm 24:3, 4, as previously noted.

Jesus reemphasized the importance of these scriptures in the presence of the scribes and Pharisees, religious rulers who were highly exacting in regard to ceremonial purity. Repeatedly they accused Him and His disciples of ignoring their ceremonial laws (Matt. 15:2; Luke 11:37). Their minds were so preoccupied with rules, restrictions, and the fear of defilement that they could not perceive the stains of selfishness and malice in their own souls.

Jesus denounced their insistence on ceremonial purity when He said:

"Woe to you, scribes and Pharisees, hypocrites! For you clean the outside of the cup and of the dish, but inside they are full of robbery and self-indulgence. You blind Pharisee, first clean the inside of the cup and of the dish, so that the outside of it may become clean also. Woe to you, scribes and Pharisees, hypocrites! For you are like whitewashed tombs which on the outside appear beautiful, but inside they are full of dead men's bones and all uncleanness. So you, too, outwardly appear righteous to men, but inwardly you are full of hypocrisy and lawlessness" (Matt. 23:25-28).

Like religious legalists today, they were big on appearance and small in authenticity. Jesus must have shocked them when He declared that happiness and the ability to see God belonged only to those who were pure in heart, not merely in outward appearance, as they thought.

A clean heart is the desire of everyone who fears God. David prayed that God would "create in me a clean heart" (Ps. 51:10). The apostle Paul said: "But the goal of our instruction is love from a pure heart and a good conscience and a sincere faith" (1 Tim. 1:5). He also urged believers to "flee from youthful lusts and pursue righteousness, faith, love and peace, with those who call on the Lord from a pure heart" (2 Tim. 2:22). Peter's entreaty to those whom he referred to as "dearly beloved" was that they "love one another fervently with a pure heart" (1 Peter 1:22, NKJV). What is this thing called purity and why is it significant in the spiritual realm?

The term *catharsis*—"to cleanse, purge, or purify"—comes from the word *katharos* that Jesus used in this beatitude. It means something that is pure not because it is already clean, but because it is being cleansed and will continue to be cleaned, as opposed to other words that describe that which is cleansed once and for all and remains so.

The English word "pure" originates from the Greek *pur* for fire and alludes to the fact that fire can consume anything that contaminates. It has come to mean something that is unmixed with any other matter, being free from dust, dirt, stain or taint, because it has been *pur*ified. Thus it represents that which is chaste, spotless, free from any form of harshness, roughness, and moral fault or guilt that vitiates, pollutes, or weakens.

The idea of purity, as preached from some pulpits in the Christian church, appears to be an impossible goal. Even children have unconsciously reached this conclusion, as demonstrated in the response of a young boy in elementary school. One day his teacher asked her class, "What is next to godliness?" Concerned about their silence, she slowly and clearly repeated, "Class, what is next to godliness?" The boy jumped to his feet and shouted nervously, "Impossible?"

Perhaps you have come to the place where you have bought into some of the current propaganda that moral purity is too high a goal to attain. If that is the case, follow along as we explore this beatitude that sets forth the gift of purity that comes with our salvation.

Jesus employed the ancient concept that the heart was the seat of our affections (Matt. 6:21; 22:37) and intellect and understanding: "For the heart of this people has become dull, with their ears they scarcely hear, and they have closed their eyes, otherwise they would see with their eyes, hear with their ears, and understand with their heart and return, and I would heal them" (Matt. 13:15).

Scripture also describes the heart as the central source of all our words and actions both good and evil (Matt. 15:19) and as the conscience (1 John 3:20, 21). By the variety of meanings we realize that when Jesus said "pure in heart" He meant far more than ceremonial or ritual purity and restraint against pollutants such as sensuality and lust. He was including all the desirable character traits and motives of the soul that is free from pride—that is not self-seeking, but is humble, unselfish, and childlike.

Human passions are the worst foes of the heart. They contaminate it with thoughts of murder, adultery, sexual promiscuity, theft, blasphemy, deceit, slander, and a host of other "works of the flesh" (Gal. 5:19, KJV). Such a heart loves the visible (seeing is believing), yet cannot see God no matter how close and personal He becomes.

To be pure in heart is equivalent to being clothed with the robe of Christ's righteousness, that fine linen God arrays the saints in (Rev. 19:8). It is to not possess what I refer to as "the *dolos* factor." This is a word that stands for "a bait or snare, guile, trickery, treachery, craftiness, false pretenses, or hypocrisy." The pure in heart avoid such attributes (John 1:47; Rev. 14:5). When the motives are pure the life will also be pure. It means that by the grace of Christ one has turned away from past mistakes and is pressing toward the mark of sinlessness in Jesus Christ (Phil. 3:12-15). Note that I said "pressing toward," to underscore the ongoing and continuous striving toward this goal. One thought that gives me great comfort is that God doesn't keep account of the times we have fallen, "for a righteous man falls seven times, [but] he rises again" (Prov. 24:16). Rather, God's interest is whether our spiritual direction is toward Him and whether we are steadfast in our persistence to get there. His focus is the fact that we have set our eyes on His face simply because we love Him.

Purity of heart by no means restricts itself to inward chastity or outward simplicity, but spills all through the life, relationships, and actions of the believer. It is good to be clean on the outside, but that purity must flow from inside. God is definitely not impressed by those who restrain themselves from enjoying life because of self-imposed and public adherence to religious rules. He finds these things detestable, especially when those same persons are privately profane in their hearts.

Some of those who insist on strictly following doctrinal truths without a balanced mixture of grace soon become contaminated with racism, genderism, and a variety of hateful thoughts against other humans. They marginalize those who do not think and believe as they do. And they are the type of people who would murder doctors who perform abortions, for the so-called noble reason of preserving human life. Jesus said that "a good tree cannot produce bad fruit, nor can a bad tree produce good fruit" (Matt. 7:18).

The inspired record of human history (which we know as the Bible) reveals that those with pure hearts have forsaken sin as a ruling principle of life (Rom. 6:12-16; 8:14-17). For example, Noah got drunk, Abraham lied, Moses and David murdered individuals who got in their way. David also committed adultery. Peter, one of the chosen disciples, cursed and denied Christ. And all of them committed such acts while pledging allegiance to God. But, unlike a host of others—such as Judas, who committed similar crimes but refused to accept responsibility—they repented and returned to fellowship with God. Sin did not rule their lives (Rom. 6:12,

13). When the Holy Spirit brought their bad behavior to their attention, they did not reject Him or neglect His instructions.

Some may protest that Moses, David, and others did those terrible things before God called them or before they came to know Him. Not so! They all committed their crimes after their positive response to the call of God and acceptance of salvation. The apostle Paul wrote years after his own dramatic conversion that he would often desire to do good, but evil was still present in his mind and sometimes won out in the internal conflict. He cried out, almost in despair, "Wretched man than I am! Who will set me free from the body of this death?" (Rom. 7:24). Then he quickly added the answer to all of our falls, faults, and failings: "Thanks be to God through Jesus Christ our Lord!" (verse 25), who delivers and saves us again and again, as often as we say, "Lord, help me!"

The truth is that one of the clearest evidences of a pure heart is our consciousness of that inner conflict. I wish those who struggle with thoughts of unworthiness or obsess over whether they are saved or not would grasp this fact. People who have committed the unpardonable sin do not go about worrying whether or not they are acceptable to God.

So how do we attain this purity when by nature the hearts of fallen humans are corrupt, deceitful, and desperately wicked (Jer. 17:9)? How can we achieve or have a pure heart?

A fourfold operation of the Holy Spirit purifies the believer. First, He instantly imparts a holy nature at rebirth or the moment of justification. God commanded that His people should "be holy; for I am holy" (Lev. 11:44). In fact, I like to emphasize that what breathing is to the natural life holiness is to the spiritual life born of the will and work of God (John 1:13; Rom. 8:5-17).

Furthermore, God has never commanded us to do that which He has not also enabled us to accomplish, so when He said, "Be holy," it was with the understanding that He had already breathed holiness into the spiritual nostrils of His born-again children. He desires that we become, in both our practice and profession of faith, that which He has already created us to be—holy. One Christian author comforts believers who might feel overwhelmed by God's expectation by promising that all His commands are our enablings (*Christ's Object Lessons,* p. 333).

Peter commented on the command to be holy:

"As obedient children, do not be conformed to the former lusts which were yours in your ignorance, but like the Holy One who called you, be holy yourselves also in your behavior [conversations]; because it is written, 'You shall be holy, for I am holy.' And if you address as Father the One who impartially judges according to each one's work, conduct yourselves in fear during the time of your stay on earth; knowing that you were not redeemed with perishable things like silver or gold from your futile way of life inherited from your forefathers, but with precious blood, as of a lamb unblemished and spotless, the blood of Christ" (1 Peter 1:14-19).

Second, the apostle Paul said, "Therefore if anyone is in Christ, [he or she] is a new creature; the old things passed away; behold, new things have come" (2 Cor. 5:17). Part of this new creation is that sin no longer reigns in our mortal bodies so that we have no choice but to obey its lusts (see Rom. 6:12-14). We also feed on the flesh (Word—John 1:14) and drink the blood (life—Lev. 17:11) of Jesus (John 6:53-58), i.e., we study the Word and imbibe His life so that by beholding we become changed into His likeness.

Third comes the process of sanctification, wherein the Holy Spirit regenerates (Titus 3:5) the believer, purging the conscience and cleansing the heart moment by moment, day by day (Acts 15:9). The apostle Paul expressed it this way: "I have been crucified with Christ; and *it is no longer I who live, but Christ lives in me;* and the life which I now live in the flesh I live by faith in the son of God, who loved me and gave Himself up for me" (Gal. 2:20).

I have come to believe that most of us have been trying to sanctify ourselves through Bible study, church attendance, and religious rituals. But Paul said that it is not us but Christ living out His life in us who accomplishes sanctification. This is a hard concept to grasp and internalize so that it becomes part of our daily practice. The operative word here is faith. By believing He is in us, then acting on what the Holy Spirit and Scripture bring to our minds and consciences, we will be sanctified daily.

While this is occurring, some of the old habits that took a long time to be established and are rooted in our past dysfunctional histories may also take a long time to be transformed or eliminated. Sometimes it may even require that the faithful believer seek the professional assistance of a Christian psychiatrist, psychologist, or counselor through whom God will work out His divinely directed acts of daily sanctification. We should not accept the old legalistic idea that a believer need only to study the Bible, read religious books, and then do what they say in order to be made whole. God also uses members of the medical profession, especially devoted counselors, to help us experience His gift of sanctification.

For example, modern psychology has determined that the human brain has three compartments. The first to develop is the visceral part. Dominant during the first two to three years of human life, it is always in a survival mode and operates by repetition—like a lizard that goes to the same spot every day to catch a fly because it found one there before. Babies, once referred to by a famous preacher as the most uncivilized beings until they are taught to live like humans, operate from this part of the brain. People who prey on others, robbing and murdering without conscience, also function largely from this part of the brain.

The second part of the brain to develop is the emotional compartment, out of which flow all the feelings of passion, fear, love, and hate. When parents or significant others do not meet childhood dependency needs, it is so painful to the developing child that by the time they are adults they close down this part of the brain. They then function primarily from the third section, the thinking brain. Some believers, who did not get their childhood developmental needs met, struggle with the demands of a practical Christian life and sometimes become quite depressed. They are likely to attribute their depression to their lack of faith, not doing the right things, or not faithfully following religious traditions, when a consultation with a Christian psychologist might reveal the truth of their early developmental deprivation. When this happens, not only is there rapid healing, but sanctification becomes a sweet experience that opens the windows of heaven and makes God's presence in the life real.

Fourth, the Holy Spirit enables and empowers us to subjugate the evil deeds of the flesh and live for God (see Rom. 8:13 and 1 Cor. 9:27). John declared:

"This is the message we have heard from Him and announce to you, that God is light, and in Him there is no darkness at all. If we say that we have fellowship with Him and yet [presently and continuously] walk in the darkness, we lie and do not practice the truth; but if we [presently and continuously] walk in the light as He Himself is in the light, we have fellowship with one another, and the blood of Jesus His Son cleanses us from all sin. If we say that we have no sin, we are deceiving ourselves, and the truth is not in us. If we confess our sins, He is faithful and righteous to forgive us our sins and to cleanse us from all unrighteousness. If we say that we have not sinned, we make Him a liar, and His word is not in us" (1 John 1:5-10).

I want to emphasize that the Bible does not teach that a pure heart means total freedom from acts of sin. This is a spiritually crippling concept of perfectionism that is popular in some circles. The Inspired Word promises that the root of sin, the home of the carnal nature, will not reign or rule in our lives anymore (Rom. 6:14). James said in his letter: "For we all stumble in many ways. If anyone does not stumble in what he says, he is a perfect man, able to bridle the whole body as well" (James 3:2). The apostle used the word *teleos* for "perfect," a term that generally signifies something or someone that has reached the end, or that which is finished, mature, and complete.

The problem is that Scripture often employs *teleos* to describe both God's perfection and human maturity. Sometimes the Bible uses the word to communicate both meanings in the same sentence. For example, a passage frequently cited to support the concept of perfectionism is one in which Jesus said, "Therefore you are to be perfect [mature], as your heavenly Father is perfect [finished, complete, with nothing to be added to Him]" (Matt. 5:48). James used the term in the latter sense, sarcastically conveying the idea of believers who think they are God, possessing goodness without the necessary reference to maturity. That sort of person sees no need for the daily doses of the Holy Spirit's cleansing ministry. They are "perfect," ready for translation, and are "so heavenly-minded that they are no earthly good."

John weighed in on this discussion again when he wrote: "My little children [in training], I am writing these things to you so *that you may not sin. And if anyone sins, we have an Advocate with the Father, Jesus Christ the righteous;* and He Himself is the propitiation for our sins; and not for ours only, but also for those of the whole world" (1 John 2:1, 2).

By now you must be bursting with the big questions: "What am I supposed to do about this? What is my role in all of this?" Our part is to confess our true condition daily, then absolutely repudiate, renounce, and forsake the self-life (Mark 8:34), considering it crucified with Christ (Rom.

6:11-14). We must walk, and keep on walking, in the path of righteousness marked out each day by the Holy Spirit. Only by accepting this gift of divine grace and allowing it to pervade our lives will we become pure in heart and able to see God.

The promises attached to the Beatitudes have both a present and future fulfillment. Let us then explore what Jesus meant when He said, Happy "are the pure in heart, for they shall see God." What is it to "see God"?

When He spoke these words, Jesus was addressing an open-air audience. If you have ever done this, as I have, you know the myriad distractions, such as the slightest cough, batting at insects, or people moving about. All of them draw attention away from the speaker. In a large, noisy, and boisterous crowd it takes an enormous amount of discipline to stay focused on speakers and what they are saying, especially in worship or other religious gatherings. It seems to me that when confronted with this situation, the Lord called His disciples and believers to be single-minded and focused in their devotion to God.

As we consider our own reputation and goals, it is very easy to be double-minded and possibly have an impure heart in God's service and worship. It is also possible to become either so pretentious or so casual and careless that we leave worship events depressed because of impure motives. Rather, we should be inspired by the powerful presence of God. The single-minded are the only people who can and will see God or get into His inner presence and find true happiness in their religion.

What exactly do we mean when we say that we want "to see a person"? Is it that we simply want to look at them with our eyes, or do we want to have an interview, to consult the person, to ask a favor or secure their opinion? "Seeing someone" is also another phrase for dating. If we go to "see" someone, we go into her or his presence to talk and exchange perspectives about a variety of subjects.

In the ancient world of Jesus, "to see" someone was a well-known metaphor for private and intimate fellowship. For example, at the beginning of His ministry, when the disciples followed Jesus and asked where He was staying, He said, "Come and see." They stayed with Him the entire day, talking and getting to know Him better (John 1:38, 39). During the last week of Jesus' life, when the Greeks in Jerusalem came to Philip and said, "Sir, we wish to see Jesus" (John 12:21), they meant that they wanted to consult Him and discuss His views on a variety of topics, especially religion. They had seen Him going about in Jerusalem, but they wanted to enter His presence and have a confidential conversation with Him. So to "see God" also means to have access to His presence and enter into intimate fellowship with Him.

Those who recognize their spiritual poverty enter the kingdom of God *now*. Those who mourn are comforted *now*, and those who are meek inherit the earth *now*. Those who hunger and thirst after righteousness are satisfied *now*, and the merciful receive mercy *now*. In the same manner the pure in heart have the privilege of seeing God—*now*. What then do we do with the verse that says, "No one has seen God at any time; the only begotten God who is in the bosom of the Father, He has explained Him" (John 1:18)? How then can we see God now? The answer is that God is seen only through the eyes of faith until we are translated into the glorious, visible kingdom at Christ's second coming (1 John 3:2; Rev. 20:4). Until then we can observe Him reflected in nature and in humans made in His image.

Only those who, through the practice of their faith, develop a heavenly vision and are able to view the world through the lens of God's Word will be able to perceive God in this world and the next. The serpent distorted Eve's view of the tree that God had instructed them not to eat from. Looking good for food, it became pleasant to her physical eyes and desirable to her spirit. Then and only then did she eat its fruit (Gen. 3:6). When the serpent said that her eyes would be opened (verse 5), he referred to the inner vision of her soul. Adam's and Eve's eyes being opened was a spiritual experience that thrust them into the knowledge of good and evil, with devastating physical and spiritual consequences for them and their descendants. The devil is always trying to open our eyes so that we can seem to be like God right now. But don't fall for it, for the reward is not only a momentary sense of pleasure; it leads to the pain of physical, if not spiritual, death.

Satan's eye-opening is really blindness. He first darkens our minds and then persuades us that intimate experience with sin will unveil a more wondrous world. The truth is that it does open our eyes, but not to happiness. It introduces us to pain, suffering, and sorrow. The horror blinds us to the grace of God the Father, the fervent, tender wooing of the Holy Spirit, and the compassion of our Savior. Satan promises to open our eyes so that we can be like God, but remember, he is a liar and the father of lies

(John 8:44). In the end he blinds us to God's will and way as well as His mercy and grace (Isa. 6:10; Eze. 12:2).

The prophet Jeremiah said: "Now hear this, O foolish and senseless people, who have eyes but do not see; who have ears but do not hear. . . . They do not say in their heart, 'Let us now fear the Lord our God, who gives rain in its season, both the autumn rain and the spring rain, who keeps for us the appointed weeks of the harvest.' Your iniquities have turned these away, and your sins have withheld good from you" (Jer. 5:21-25).

Since we have all sinned (Ps. 51:5; Rom. 3:23), we are also all blind from birth. How then can we, the blind, see God? Not until the new birth divinely opens our eyes.

First, we can see God through rebirth by faith—through grace. Only those born again of the Spirit and water are able to enter the kingdom of God and see Him (John 3:3-6).

Second, we will see God when we have a close, intimate relationship with Him (Rom. 8). When you read this biblical passage, include your name in it so that it becomes personal and discover the spiritual blessings available to you.

Third, we *will* see God when we "draw near to God and He will draw near to you. Cleanse your hands, you sinners; and purify your hearts, you double-minded. Be miserable and mourn and weep; let your laughter be turned into mourning and your joy to gloom. Humble yourselves in the presence of the Lord, and He will exalt you" (James 4:8-10).

Fourth, we can see God when we cultivate a singleness of eye, for no one can serve two masters. "The eye is the lamp of the body; so then if your eye is clear, your whole body will be full of light. But if your eye is bad, your whole body will be full of darkness. If then the light that is in you is darkness, how great is the darkness!" (Matt. 6:22, 23).

Fifth, we must keep our eyes, the windows of our soul, constantly clean. Just as we diligently clean our eyeglasses and contact lenses with special cloths and chemicals to ensure clear vision and no contamination or inflammation, so we must clean our spiritual eyes with the Word of God. The Scriptures must be the lens through which we look at God, His world, and the kingdom of God (1 Cor. 13:12).

Finally, we must want to see Jesus more than anything else in the world, for when we have seen Him we have observed the Father (John 14:7).

Have you ever tried to decide which eye to look into when you were interacting with a visually impaired person whose eyes are crossed? It is very distracting! Far too many Christians are spiritually wall-eyed. They are trying to focus one eye on heavenly promises and the other eye on worldly pleasures of sin. The only way we can be truly focused is to live by God's principles and make Him first in our lives by allowing Jesus to take up permanent residence in our hearts. Then not only will we be able to see our Father in heaven, but also we will see Him on earth—in our spiritual brothers and sisters.

When we are physically attracted to someone, or in love, our pupils dilate. Perhaps this is the phenomenon that led to the phrase "seeing the light" or "seeing through rose-colored glasses." When we view God through eyes of faith, it fills our soul eyes with His light and love, and in the process we can't help viewing His world and children as He does. How precious and beautiful they are!

In order to enjoy the benefits of this beatitude, we must draw close to God with a sincere heart. No matter how good our vision, we cannot see natural objects at a vast distance. In the same way, we cannot discern spiritual things by standing far from God. That's why God is always seeking intimate relations with His people.

An intimate divine association provides two immediate and important benefits. First, we enjoy the twofold work of justification and sanctification as we anticipate glorification at the Second Coming. Second, we enjoy eternal life starting now (John 3:36) and escape the condemnation of the final judgment (John 5:24).

Happy are the pure in heart, for they shall see God *now,* in this present world, as we wait to live eternally with Him in the next!

CHAPTER

8

Portrait of a Peacemaker

"Happy the peacemakers—because they shall be called Sons of God."
Matthew 5:9, YLT.

It has been almost five decades since I left my small sun-drenched paradise nestled in the heart of the Caribbean. Since then, I have traveled to more than 40 countries, seen the first human being walk on the moon, and admired the power of technology, especially the Internet. During those years I have spoken to more than 25,000 people at one time and as few as 10 in one event. I have drunk deeply—to the point of intoxication—from the cup of increased knowledge in these last days.

One thing that used to amaze me was the idea of rainmaking. It flabbergasted me when I first discovered its existence—and the fact that so many seemed to take it for granted. But for me it seemed marvelous. During those early years after I left my island home I found myself astounded by the ingenuity of pilots who flew into rainless clouds, seeded them with chemicals, and—voilà—rain. As a result, for some years the rainmaker was my hero. They seemed, I thought, able to do that which God Himself sometimes could not.

Like rainmakers, peacemakers are those who create peace in places and situations in which there is otherwise not the remotest chance of anything other than war, tumult, and conflict. They bring real solutions to our restlessness, anger, and assault upon God, ourselves, and others.

As Christians, when we survey the world, to our dismay we discover that all nature is in convulsion. If we should begin with our own fallen nature, as we ought, we will note that it nourishes distorted imagination, disobedience, disorder, and a host of perverted passions. Without God in residence to order our affairs daily, these insurgent passions dethrone reason and rule us. Not only do the broken shards of our existence injure us, but with our lives out of control we hurt others who do not come up to our expectations.

Thus conflict rages not only between nations but also between individuals and even within ourselves. No matter how much peace our attempts at political or economic regeneration might produce, it does not last. New struggles quickly break out. The warfare never ceases.

As long as the great controversy between good and evil continues, heaven and earth will struggle against each other. The conflict will endure until its conclusion in the lake of fire (Rev. 20:13, 14). The human race is in rebellion against God. Some openly resist Him, while others mask their hostility with hypocrisy. We desperately need a peacemaker. Thank God He has come in the person of Jesus Christ our Lord, who declared that peacemakers are not only happy, but are called, named, and recognized as the sons and daughters of God.

Just as those who hunger and thirst after righteousness are filled, those who mourn are comforted, and the pure in heart see God, so also peacemakers establish real peace. Only those who are able, by the power and presence of the Holy Spirit, to cry authentically from their heart, "Abba! Father!" are able to do God's work—His way.

It is significant that Jesus said "peacemaker" and not "peaceable person" when He gave this beatitude, because there is a distinct difference between them. The peaceable merely help others to feel comfortable in awkward situations, even if it means compromising principles and abandoning standards. They accept things as they are and generally follow the path of least resistance, putting expediency before principle. As they drift with the current they tend to honor mediocrity, procrastinate, and have no real goals or destination. And under the shelter of their so-called peace all manners of abuses thrive alongside egotism, exhibitionism, and self-promotion.

A perverted Christian perception of meekness considers being peaceable as a winning characteristic because it willingly accepts circumstances as they are, often reasoning that it is God's will. Those who tolerate the kind of peaceable nature we have been discussing seem to believe that

Christians should sit back and fold their hands while sin festers in the dark, injustice reigns, and oppression, prejudice, and deceit stir up conflict. They have even suggested that being this kind of peaceable is what Jesus meant when He said "peacemaker."

But God is not a "peaceable" person in this sense, and neither are His children. His portrait of a peacemaker is that of one who hates compromise. Although God does not tempt anyone (James 1:13), He is a peacemaker who sometimes expresses His love by leading us into and through temptation's territory. Afterward we can know that we are strong Christians who can weather the storms by holding on to His hand. He often allows suffering and permits sin to discipline His children.

God calls us to be peacemakers as was Jesus Christ. A peacemaker of a different kind, He declared that He had come to bring a sword (i.e., the Word of God [Heb. 4:12]) and not peace as they knew it (Matt. 10:34). He disturbed the status quo with His interpretation of the Word of God and with His radical life and death. Jesus established that a peacemaker is one who is nailed on the cross of utter surrender, sacrifice, obedience, and absolute loyalty to our heavenly Father. His influence created a whirlwind of infinite desire and unsatisfied longing for God in human hearts. As a result, those who went out in His name turned the world upside down, not with swords and plowshares, but with love and compassion.

No one who truly has His Spirit and the peace that He has given can be a peacemaker until they have experienced betrayal, knelt in their own Gethsemane, then later struggled and fell under the weight of the cross to their own place of crucifixion. All who disturb traditions, conventions, and human formalities face the threat of being persecuted for righteousness' sake. They may be reviled or have all manner of evil spoken and written against them. As guardians of God's will and Word, they fight for the faith against every disruptive element of this world.

God's peacemakers are like Athena, the goddess of wisdom, whom the ancient Greeks chose as their protector. When they carved her image they portrayed her bearing a spear in one hand and an olive branch in the other. Peacemakers are fearless men and women whose divine connection empowers them to speak boldly for God whenever necessary or to welcome little children to sit on their laps.

Although every peacemaker is a fighter, not every fighter is a peacemaker. True, divinely appointed and anointed peacemakers do not live for themselves (see Matt. 26:52-54 and 2 Cor. 5:15), but fight for God's sake. No one can be a peacemaker unless they have God's peace in their heart. God's warfare seeks to save and not to destroy, to provide pardon and not to avenge, to establish mercy and not merely justice.

The indignation of a peacemaker is an empathy purged of revenge and aggressiveness. It hears the still small voice, the wooing whispers, of God above every tumult, saying, "The Lord is in His holy temple. Let all the earth keep silence before Him" (Hab. 2:20). A peacemaker is one whose current of life in Christ flows from the fountain of forgiveness.

"Happy [are] the peacemakers," for "they shall be called Sons of God." They partake of the nature of the Spirit of peace and find rest in the great High Priest who was "tempted in all things as we are, yet without sin" (Heb. 4:15).

We live in a world that desperately needs peace—not just the temporary halt to national crises, international conflicts, and terrorist attacks, but that inner peace that passes all understanding (Phil. 4:7). As we explore the wonderful call and opportunity to be sons and daughters of God in this beatitude, we will also discover practical steps and methods to becoming peacemakers.

Many of God's people in New Testament times expected that the promised Messiah would conduct an unprecedented and uninterrupted series of wars against their enemies until they had completely destroyed all other nations and totally subjugated their peoples. Then His chosen people would be independent again. A great human warrior appointed by God would bring about a national deliverance instead of the God-man's redemption from the dominion of evil.

As a result, as they read the experiences of their forebears, especially in the book of Joshua, they assumed they would fight similar battles. But God had a different plan for their lives. In His great mission against sin He sent them Immanuel, "God with us" (Matt. 1:23). To their great disappointment, He was not what they anticipated. The religious leaders expected a human hero to free them from foreign oppression. But when God Himself came as a divine Savior to deliver the world from sin and spiritual oppression, they got what they needed, not what they wanted—and were they angry! So the religious leaders rejected Him (John 1:11) and sought to destroy His credibility with the people as they plotted to kill Him.

The people of Jesus' time had to contend with the horrible enmity that sin had brought into the world. Like every generation since the Fall, they struggled with malice and envy (Titus 3:3). If there was ever a time anyone needed the presence of peacemakers, it was then (as is still the case). The political leaders thought the answer was more insurrections and assassinations, which not only exacerbated the problems but increased persecution of their own people by the Roman rulers.

Imagine, then, how hopeful it must have been to the multitude on the mountainside when Jesus announced that in His kingdom there was happiness for those who were deliberate, intentional peacemakers. That those who actively tried to make peace would be called the children of God. But that fact scandalized the national leaders, who took pride in their Abrahamic heritage.

It would be helpful to take note of the original meaning of the word "peacemaker" in order to understand and appreciate fully what Jesus meant and what the people heard when He said, "Happy [are] the peacemakers." The word *eirenopoios* ("peacemaker") is a combination of two words: *eirene,* "peace," and *poios,* "maker." The first word describes a harmonious relationship, especially that which exists between God and humans as a result of the impact of the gospel (2 Cor. 5:14-21). It means friendliness and freedom from any kind of disruption or molestation of evil in the orderly functions of the church and state (something, sadly, I have never seen in my lifetime).

The corresponding word in Hebrew is *shalom,* which adds a further dimension to the Greek meaning, such as "completeness, soundness, wholeness, prosperity, and the condition of well-being."

Poios, "maker," is the second part of the Greek word for peacemaker. It gives a definitive action to the accomplishment of peace, emphasizing that peace is not attained by osmosis or threats, but by a deliberate, proactive plan of action. To "make" something also requires creative action and behavior that produces results.

When we put all of this together, we discover that Jesus was not talking about a person who avoids all conflicts or confrontations and is laid-back, easygoing, and relaxed about everything. He was describing peacemakers who are the epitome of grace and love plus judgment and justice—as He is.

During His earthly sojourn Jesus could have summoned 10,000 angels to bring instant national peace from the oppressive hand of the Roman rulers. With a blink of an eye He could have delivered the poor people from the heavy-handed regulations imposed on them by the religious leaders. But He never employed solutions and methods that would only alleviate the symptoms. He did radical surgery by eliminating the cancer of unrest and conflicts at the root of sin. As He delineated the seventh pillar in His kingdom of grace He offered the people something much more important and eternal than the quick, bloody solutions proposed by political zealots. Jesus assured His hearers that they could all be peacemakers, not through the use of political power but by bringing men and women into harmony and peace with God—and not only then or now, but for all eternity.

Fallen human minds are always at enmity with God (Rom. 8:7), but Jesus Christ, the divine peacemaker, came to show us that God is not our enemy. So let us take a closer look at His life to learn how to become like our Elder Brother and Savior.

First, Jesus did nothing without the guidance of the Father (John 3:17; 5:30-36). This is really an important point for the believer who wants to be a peacemaker. Not only must we know who we are in Christ, but we must also know whose we are as we wholly follow our heavenly Father's instructions. We must be called and sent by God with the purpose of building up and not tearing down His people, work, and world. Too often we take it upon ourselves to make peace before the Holy Spirit has yet sent us and thus find ourselves in the center of conflicts and disruptions because we moved before we had God's approval to act.

I once had a woman come to me to apologize for things I did not even know she thought or felt about me in her heart. After unloading some of the harshest things—things that she should have really left unsaid—she insisted that I forgive her. When she finished, she sighed with relief and departed, unmindful or unmoved by the fact that her words had badly wounded me. The painful encounter left me numb for days. I did not need to know she thought those things about me. Had she been motivated by the Holy Spirit, I believe she would have been more compassionate, even as she said things that I was not ready to hear.

Months later I discovered that she was against women in ministry and seized the opportunity to say, under the guise of seeking forgiveness, what she did not have the courage to express otherwise. I had to struggle against a variety of hostile thoughts for a long time before I was able to accept her as a sister in Christ.

The second notable characteristic in Jesus' way of attaining peace was that our great Peacemaker said we are to be like Him. "A disciple is not above his teacher, nor a slave above his master. It is enough for the disciple that he become like his teacher, and the slave like his master" (Matt. 10:24, 25).

This means that a disciple of Jesus who is a true peacemaker does not bring peace as we know it, but a sword (verse 34). Greek has two words for sword: *romphaia,* a long, large Thracian weapon and instrument of pain and war, and *machaira,* the word Jesus used. The latter was a small, short sword or dagger, possibly a knife that the men of that day used to sacrifice and skin animals as well as to trim their own beards. It was also the knife one employed to peel fruits, or like the physician's scalpel, to cut carefully into the flesh of a person undergoing surgery. By the way, this is the same weapon that the crowd brought (Matt. 26:47) and that Peter used to cut off the ear of the high priest's servant when Judas betrayed Jesus and the Temple guards arrested Him in Gethsemane (verses 51, 52).

Jesus employed this word metaphorically and by metonymy to denote an instrument of life, not death, that also represents the Word of God (Eph. 6:17; Heb. 5:12). It is a sharp two-edged sword (knife) that cuts both ways: to conversion and to condemnation. Additionally, it was also one of the few implements owned and used by the common people. So imagine the relief they must have felt to note that in order for them to be a peacemaker Jesus was empowering them to use something that they already possessed. Through God's grace they would bring healing to the heart, mind, and body of ailing humanity.

How, then, do we accomplish this peacemaking work? First, let me make it clear that it is not an easy task. It is not the kind of approach that is more cowardice and selfishness than peace. Nor is it the peace at any price popularly promoted among some Christians today. Instead, it works through a great and divine force that must be administered with wisdom. So powerful is this inward discipline that God alone gives it to believers (John 14:27).

The apostle James declared: "But the wisdom from above is first pure, then peaceable, gentle, reasonable, full of mercy and good fruits, unwavering, without hypocrisy" (James 3:17). God's version of peacemaking is to be merciful and kind to a known enemy. It does not take revenge, but leaves it to the Lord, who said, "Vengeance is Mine, I will repay" (Rom. 12:19; cf. Deut. 32:35, 36; 2 Kings 6:22).

The peacemakers who trust God to take care of wrongs can then operate without partiality and hypocrisy as they actively seek peace (Heb. 12:14, 15). This is the kind of son and daughter of God whom the world really needs now. All creation is groaning and eagerly awaiting the revelation of these peacemakers and the advent of this peace (see Rom. 8:19-22).

It is important to notice that after His resurrection one of the first things Jesus did for His fear-filled disciples was to say, "Peace be with you" (John 20:26). Earlier He had declared, "Peace I leave with you; My peace I give to you; not as the world gives do I give to you. Do not let your heart be troubled, nor let it be fearful" (John 14:27).

As long as we have Jesus we will have the Comforter (John 14:16, 26) and will be peacemakers, sons and daughters of God to whom the apostle Paul said, "Now may the Lord of peace Himself continually grant you peace in every circumstance. The Lord be with you all!" (2 Thess. 5:16). If we are to function successfully as peacemakers, we must impart the peace of Christ in all circumstances of life.

"Therefore, having been justified by faith, we have peace with God through our Lord Jesus Christ," Paul stated (Rom. 5:1). He commanded Christians to be at peace with one another (1 Thess. 3:13). We are to pray for peace and take a constructive interest in activities that contribute to peace wherever we live. "See how great a love the Father has bestowed on us, that we would be called children of God; and such we are. For this reason the world does not know us, because it did not know Him. Beloved, now we are children of God, and it has not appeared as yet what we will be. We know that when He appears, we will be like Him, because we will see Him just as He is. And everyone who has this hope fixed on Him purifies himself, just as He is pure" (1 John 3:1-3).

What does it mean to be a son or daughter of God? I believe that when Jesus said we are called the children of God, He had in mind that after being justified, or born again, we are literally, legally, and spiritually His children (John 1:12, 13; 1 John 3:7-10). I have written extensively on this concept in my book *Anticipation* (see chapter 7, "Don't Give Up!" [pp. 191-222]), but let me show you something spectacular about being the child of God.

In the time of Jesus if a Jewish family lost all its wealth and prosperity, they could sell their freeborn children, along with themselves, into slavery. However, according to the Roman law, children who were formerly slaves and then redeemed could not be sold again into slavery. To ensure this, they issued a document called the *exousia,* which functioned much as a legal certificate of adoption does today. The word also means legal right or authority—in this case, from God.

John employed this same word when explaining the legitimacy and authenticity of the heritage of the children of God. "But as many as received Him [Jesus Christ], to them He gave the right *[exousian]* to become children of God, even to those who believe in His name, who were born, not of blood nor of the will of the flesh nor of the will of man, but of God" (John 1:12, 13).

Paul expanded on the concept of adoption in his Epistles (see Rom. 8:15, 23; 9:4; Gal. 4:5; Eph. 1:5). Also he emphasized spiritual rebirth (Rom. 8:14-17). Why did the New Testament writers underscore both the rebirth and adoption? The biblical writers, who themselves had the opportunity to be personally trained by God Himself in the living person of Jesus Christ, wanted to assure us that the Lord took every precaution to doubly ensure that we are His children.

First Jesus Christ, our goel (kinsman redeemer [Lev. 25:25; Ruth 4:4; Jer. 32:6-12]), bought us back from our slave master, Satan (1 Cor. 6:19, 20). God also caused us to be born-again children (John 3:3-5). Then He gave us a certificate of adoption in case the enemy of our souls should try to persuade us that we really are not part of His kingdom and that we really do not belong to Him. Should the devil ever try to convince us that God might run out of resources and have to sell us into slavery (our carnal nature) again, we have this spiritual certificate of adoption. We can be assured of our heritage, legal right, and authority as sons and daughters of the Most High (see Revelation 12:10, in which exousia is translated as "authority"). If we are to be slaves again, we'll be slaves of God, as Paul states repeatedly in his Epistles.

Not only are we bought by the blood of the Lamb and are spiritually born again into the divine family; we have been legally adopted by the Holy Trinity. We can never be sold again into the slavery of sin. I hope that not one of us would be foolish enough to return willingly to that shame-based life! Let us, therefore, be very careful not to slip back into that horrible state of unrest we endured before Christ came into our lives and gave us peace. In one of his songs, Steven Curtis Chapman charges us to remember our chains, but when we do, we are also to remember that they are gone. Let us not be like some slaves who continued to live as if they were chained long after the fetters had been broken and removed.

Peace is rare. Ask the people who live in such hot spots as the Middle East. Some historians estimate that our world has been at peace only about 8 percent of the time since the beginning of recorded time. They estimate that more than 8,000 treaties have been broken in at least the Western world during this period.

God said that many would proclaim, "'Peace, peace,' but there is no peace" (Jer. 6:14). And so it is unless we accept the Prince of Peace, Jesus Christ, into our hearts and lives. When we do, we will be happy peacemakers who are called the children of God. Undisturbed by the presence, power, or promised penalty of sin, we will be at peace.

Once two artists received a commission to paint a picture of perfect peace. On his canvas the first artist depicted a carefree boy sitting in a boat on a placid lake without a single ripple disturbing the surface. The lake was peacefully nestled in a valley near a range of rugged mountains.

For his scene the other painter chose a raging waterfall with turbulent winds whipping the spray high above the river. On a fragile limb bending over the foam, overhanging the swirling water, sat a bird in its nest. She seemed serene as she sat peacefully brooding over her eggs while sprays from the thundering waterfall threatened to wash away her abode. The little bird sat there tranquilly, unafraid of the dangerous sprays from the roaring falls because she knew that in that setting she was absolutely safe from predators. The very thing that seemed to threaten her safety actually shielded and protected her. You see, life in Christ is all about perspective!

The Holy Spirit is our limb hanging over the storms of life. Such storms break upon us unexpectedly and often with devastating results. We must climb up and nestle into the bosom of Jesus Christ, our nest over troubled waters. He alone can rebuke the storm, saying, "Peace, be still" (or as it is recorded in the Greek, "Shut up!"), and those fierce gales of storm will become perfectly calm (Mark 4:35-41).

Real peacemakers are those who, like the bird, remain calm in Jesus Christ even in the midst of trials and temptations. God promises that He will make even our enemies to be at peace with us (Prov. 16:7). The true peacemakers are, above all things, those who have tranquillity. Turbulence, destruction, and fearfulness may surround them, but they know that all is under control and operating in balance because they, like Jesus Christ, are sons and daughters of God.

From now on, just call me a peacemaker. Why? Because I am a born-again, baptized-in-the-blood-of-the-Lamb child of God. I'm so glad you are too.

CHAPTER

The Joy of the Hard Way

"Happy those persecuted for righteousness' sake—because theirs is the reign of the heavens." Matthew 5:10, YLT.

On January 30, 1973, Patrice Tamao of Santo Domingo, Dominican Republic, had himself nailed to a cross in a public ceremony. He attracted worldwide attention for his unusual behavior. News reports announced that he planned his radical act "as a sacrifice for world peace and understanding among" all people. As thousands watched on television, six-inch stainless steel nails were hammered into his hands and feet.

It was Tamao's plan to remain on the cross for 48 hours, but he was unable to accomplish his goal. After only 20 hours this ambitious man had to cut his voluntary crucifixion short because of an inflamed infection in his right foot. The media reaction over his attempt resembled nothing less than a shark attack and feeding frenzy. The next morning one newspaper article boasted the following headline: "Crucifixion for Peace Falls Short."

The incident powerfully reminds us that only the crucifixion of Jesus Christ can bring real peace into the world. But that peace for the world as a whole is yet future. Until then, the winds of affliction or adversity will sweep through everyone's life, often through persecution perpetrated by Satan, God's forever enemy.

I once read that if the world has nothing to say against a Christian, it is because Christ has nothing to say for and through that individual. Life is so good and easy for most Christians in the Western Hemisphere that the word "persecution" has little or no meaning for many. Quite a few of us do not expect any turbulence on life's journey. When it does come, however, some curse God and argue vociferously with Him for allowing sudden calamities or unexpected adversities (whether of their own or others' making) to interrupt their charmed existence. Yet come they do. Thus the questions: Have you ever been persecuted for doing the right thing? Did you like it? Of course not! We are Christians, not masochists! But what if you were persecuted because of your faith in Jesus Christ in these supposedly gentler and more humane times—how would you respond or react?

I would hope that if I should face persecution for my faith I would conduct myself as did Obediah Holmes, a resident of Massachusetts in 1651. It was reported that he held a prayer meeting in his home during the time of a statewide ban against religious gatherings in private homes. When the authorities heard about it, they notified the governor, who ordered Holmes to be publicly whipped as a stern message to him and others who might conduct similar meetings. So severe was the beating that for days Holmes could not lie or sit down. The best he could do was to rest on the tips of his elbows and knees, even though such pressure on his muscles added to his discomfort and pain. Yet when the last lash had fallen on his bleeding body, onlookers were surprised to hear him say, as he forced a smile through his bloodstained lips, "Gentlemen, you have whipped me with roses! How sweet is the scent of persecution!"

A history of the lives, sufferings, and deaths of early Christian martyrs provides some of the most powerful testimonies of endurance under persecution.

James the son of Zebedee was the first disciple to be martyred by Herod Agrippa (Acts 12:1, 2). The terse report does not convey its full trauma. Luke simply states that he, along with others, was arrested and mistreated before Herod's henchmen cruelly beheaded him.

Philip, born in Bethsaida, was the first one called by Jesus to follow Him and be His disciple (John 1:43). After Christ's ascension Philip spent his time ministering to the people in Upper Asia, where he apparently suffered martyrdom at Heliopolis in Phrygia. Tradition says he was scourged, thrown into prison, and crucified in A.D. 54.

Matthew, the tax gatherer, wrote the Gospel bearing his name. He, along with the other disciples, obeyed the instructions of Jesus to flee

Jerusalem when they saw the abomination of desolation taking place about 30 years later. Tradition states that the apostle went to Parthia and Ethiopia to spread the good news of Jesus Christ. While he was in Ethiopia, in the city of Nadabah, sometime in A.D. 60, an angry mob murdered him.

James the Less, so called by the early Church Fathers, was reportedly the eldest son of Joseph and stepbrother of Jesus; a pillar of the church in Jerusalem (Gal. 2:9); and the author of the New Testament book bearing his name. He was martyred at the age of 94. Tradition says that after a mob severely beat him, they then used a fuller's club, an instrument for refining woolen cloth, to bash in his head.

Matthias, whose name means "gift of Yahweh," and of whom little is known except that he was elected at Pentecost to fill the vacancy created by Judas Iscariot, was apparently stoned to death and beheaded in Jerusalem.

Andrew, whose name means "manly" and was the brother of Peter, died a manly death. He preached the gospel to many Asiatic nations before being cruelly crucified at Edessa. The cross on which he died was shaped like an X, with two ends planted in the ground. The device was later popularized as an instrument of torture for Christians. Many martyrs pleaded with their persecutors for the privilege of suffering on what they called Saint Andrew's cross.

Peter's history and his story are perhaps the best known among the disciples. Jesus actually told him how he would die as a martyr when He said to him, "When you grow old, you will stretch out your hands and someone else will gird you, and bring you where you do not wish to go" (John 21:18). Many believe that he died in Rome. After being arrested, he was blindfolded and led to the place of crucifixion, where his arms and legs were stretched out until his muscles separated from their joints. Instead of the usual upright position on the cross, Peter requested to be placed upside down, because he said he was unworthy to be crucified in the same manner as his Lord Jesus Christ.

Bartholomew, a disciple of whom Scripture says little, later preached the gospel in many countries. Tradition claims that he translated the Gospel of Matthew into the language of India, where he was cruelly beaten and then crucified.

Thomas, also called Didymus (meaning "twofold" or "twins"), perhaps because he was the surviving sibling of twins, is often cited by

Christian preachers today as one who "doubted" (John 20:25). Yet a closer examination of that passage reveals that he was the first person to recognize that Jesus is God. While the other disciples slowly came to this realization only years after Jesus' ascension, Thomas acknowledged His divinity immediately after His resurrection. On that occasion he addressed Jesus as YHWH when he referred to Him as "Lord" by using the Hebrew *Adonai,* a word formed from the omitted vowels of the sacred tetragrammaton (verse 28). Thomas apparently preached the gospel in Parthia and India, where, according to one tradition, he excited the rage of pagan priests, who murdered him.

Judas the son of James (Luke 6:16; Acts 1:13), also called Thaddaeus (Matt. 10:3; Mark 3:18), was crucified at Edessa in A.D. 72.

Simon the Zealot was a political activist before his association with Jesus as a disciple. After he fled Jerusalem during the Roman siege of A.D. 70, tradition says that he traveled to Africa and Britain, where he fearlessly preached the gospel and was crucified in Britain in A.D. 74.

John the "beloved disciple," brother of James, the first apostle martyred, left us the rich legacy of the book of Revelation. The Romans arrested him in Ephesus and extradited him to Rome, where the emperor Domitian had him cast into a cauldron of boiling oil. The apostle escaped without injury through a miracle. The emperor then had him banished to the Isle of Patmos. But that which the enemy meant for evil, God used for the good of His people and honor of His name. The Lord sent to His faithful servant visions of things to come, later recorded in the book of Revelation, on the very island of his exile. Apparently John was the only apostle who escaped a violent death. After the death of Domitian, John was released, and returned to Ephesus, where he lived until he was laid to a peaceful rest.

John Mark and members of his family may have operated the first house church in Jerusalem after Pentecost. Converted by Peter, he diligently served the apostle as an amanuensis, or secretary, and received first-hand from him the testimonies reported in his version of the Gospels. Some believe that Mark was describing himself in the story that only he records about the young man who lost his clothing during the arrest of Jesus (Mark 14:51, 52). He was acquainted with conflict (Acts 12:25; 15:37-39), but nothing like the merciless treatment tradition says he suffered in Alexandria. There, during worship of their god, Serapis, whom Mark publicly denounced in his preaching, the angry people grabbed him and dragged him along their rough, unpaved streets until it had worn all his skin from his body. Then they hacked him into pieces.

The apostle Paul started out as a persecutor of the fledgling church (Acts 8:1-3), but dramatically accepted a call from Christ on the road to Damascus (Acts 9:1-9). By his own admission he suffered tremendously for preaching the gospel (2 Cor. 11:23-27). Nero's soldiers led him outside the city of Rome, where he prayed and gave his neck to the sword.

Luke had been a capable physician who cared for the bodies of men and women to preserve their natural lives. Converted to Christ, he then spent the rest of his life as a devoted evangelist caring for spiritual lives. Traveling with Paul to many countries where they ministered together, he authored the New Testament books of Luke and the Acts of the Apostles. Extrabiblical history reports that Luke was eventually hanged on an olive tree in Greece before a multitude of people who accepted his message of God's grace.

These men—and many women, such as Mary (Rom. 16:6), the apostle Junias (verse 7), Julia and Olympas (verse 15)—formed part of a great host of witnesses who suffered and died for their faith. Many stories of these martyrs, especially those of women, did not get preserved, but those that were preserved give us reason to conclude that the foundation of Christianity was laid on the bedrock of the blood of suffering and dying saints. For the hope of experiencing the happiness promised by their Lord, they endured tribulation and lived at peace with God, content with their condition (Phil. 4:11). Hebrews 11 paints a powerful portrait of believers who, even though they endured persecution, died happy knowing that they were members of the kingdom of heaven (2 Tim. 4:8).

There has never been a time, from the Fall of humanity into sin to the present, that God's people have not suffered persecution. In fact, in the very first story of human family interaction, we discover persecution (Gen. 4:1-8). This first persecution of a righteous person involved two siblings. Cain became angry because God regarded Abel's offering more than his, a reaction that continues to rear its ugly head among believers today.

Notice that Abel perished at the hand of his own worshiping, believing, professing-faith-in-God brother—not a stranger. This demonstrates that a real loyalty to God will always bring persecution. The majority of people who persecute believers will be and often are professed spiritual brothers and sisters who claim to be children of the one God.

Historians estimate that more than 50 million Christians died for their faith during the period known as the Dark Ages (approximately sixth to eleventh centuries). Perhaps a million Christians perished after the Communists seized China. Unnumbered and unsung millions have died as martyrs in the revolutions and civil wars in South America and Africa. Many Christians still face persecution and death by torture for their faith in Christ. At the end of the twentieth century the watchdog group Amnesty International announced that the persecution of Christians around the world had increased significantly, with every sign of its continuance in the twenty-first century.

It is very important to establish immediately that not everyone who experiences persecution suffers for righteousness' sake. Political martyrs are numerous. Self-made so-called Christian martyrs are a dime a dozen these days. Sometimes, if we should analyze some of those claiming to be persecuted, we would discover that their suffering resulted more from a cantankerous disposition than from any bold championship of principles and beliefs or from the opposition of nonbelievers. Those who court persecution by tactlessness and religious bigotry only bring Christianity into disrepute. Others stir up controversy and bitterness over humanly constructed doctrines and standards irrelevant to salvation. As a result they arouse the ire of those they denounce. Their focus is not on the kingdom of heaven or righteousness, but on their own concerns.

Sometimes no one knows about the trials and tribulations of many Christians because stories of true persecution for righteousness' sake do not reach the daily news. They often die with the martyrs. For example, years ago when I was a student in seminary I spent my vacations working with an evangelist during a summer-long series of meetings in a tent. My Bible instructor partner and I had the privilege of sharing the good news with a large woman who was married to a stripling of a man. When he discovered that she was receiving Bible studies, he increased his abuse to include regular beatings. She kept her secret of domestic violence and suffered unspeakably for persisting with the Bible studies. On one occasion, in a fit of demonic rage, her husband punched her in one eye and broke every blood vessel in it; she would forever have blurred vision in that eye. When we discovered the details of her suffering, we expected her to stop the studies, but instead she made plans to meet at 3:00 in the morning under a street lamp near her home while her husband slept.

The day she was to be baptized came. Her husband secretly followed us to the location of the big baptism. There he appeared with a gun in his hand, threatening to take her life if she dared to defy him and get into the water. My Bible study partner and I foolishly jumped in front of her to protect her from him.

Afterward we concluded that in addition to fulfilling God's promise to look after fools and orphans, the Holy Spirit restrained that angry man. There we were, two unarmed women, literally swallowed up in folds of flesh and the clothing of that buxom woman while screaming, "You have to go through us to get to her!"

This woman, who was persecuted for righteousness' sake, was baptized that day knowing that if her husband did not keep his word to kill her then, he would severely beat and perhaps murder her at home. Instead of running away, as I would have done, she returned home, praying and believing that God would protect her—and He did. More than a year later she called to let me know that her husband had finally surrendered his life to Christ and would be baptized that day. They both continue to serve God as leaders of their church and as upstanding members of their community.

It is not always the antagonism of those who reject Christian values that we have to fear. Most often it is the wrath of believers who cannot control their own lives and who become writers of anonymous poison pen letters or use modern technology such as videos and the Internet to parade their lies and persecute God's faithful servants. Others are convinced that their doctrines and religious views are the only correct ones. They persecute the people of God who are not of their fellowship, erroneously believing they are doing so for His sake.

Selfishness and other forms of subtle evil also often motivate those who seek position and political power in both local congregations and denominational hierarchy, leading to malice, conflict, and disruptive behavior in many communities of faith. Thank God, however, some are still willing to give up their own rights, and instead of justifying or vindicating themselves, they endure persecution for no other reason than their total commitment to Jesus Christ.

While "righteousness" is the character or quality of being right or just, the word "persecute" literally means to put to flight, to drive away, to pursue. The persecuted are harassed in a manner to cause injury. Treated like wild beasts, they may lose family, friends, property, dignity, and reputation. Some find themselves driven to destitution for their faith in God before death becomes a welcome escape.

It seems incongruous for Jesus to use the word "happy" in the same sentence with the word "persecute." So I am delighted to discover that Jesus did not expect the persecuted to be "happy" during such trials and trauma, but committed Himself to provide happiness for them *after* their ordeals.

Jesus declared: "Happy [are] those *persecuted* for righteousness' sake," for "theirs is the reign of the heavens." This means that the promised happiness comes after the persecution, for which I am very grateful, because I don't want to feel guilty when I groan and hurt during such painful experiences. It is such a blessing to know that it was "for the *joy set before Him*"—not *during* the ordeal—that Jesus "endured the cross, despising the shame" (Heb. 12:2). Scripture does not record that He enjoyed the hostility and humiliation.

I applaud those early martyrs such as Polycarp, bishop of Smyrna, who suffered martyrdom in A.D. 155. When the authorities brought him to the stake, he demanded to stand without the usual restraints. "Let me alone," he protested, "for He who gave me strength to come to the fire will give me patience to endure the flames."

A church council arrested, condemned, and sentenced John Huss, the courageous pastor of Prague, to be burned in 1415. When he heard his sentence pronounced, he fell to his knees and prayed, "Lord Jesus, forgive my enemies." Chained to the stake, he prayed, "In Thee, O Lord, do I put my trust; let me never be ashamed." Then the flames snuffed out the life of the one known as the "Morning Star of the Reformation."

In spite of such courageous forerunners of our faith, I will not add to the suffering of today's saints any requirement to be composed and happy in the heat of persecution. But there can be joy—joy that results from grace operating under duress. It comes only to those who walk along the narrow way of righteousness. All who have been converted have had this personal experience. When we begin to separate from sin and darkness and enter the marvelous life of God's grace by laying aside the old self and putting on the new (Col. 3:1-17), family and friends often become antagonistic foes. We feel a loss of belonging, no longer accepted in our old world and too awkward to be comfortable in the new. Yet deep inside ourselves we still experience a peace, a sense of finally finding our true selves and knowing that God is with us. As we discover our true identity and being, no word except "happiness" can adequately portray this experience.

Such coveted happiness comes through the hardness of life only to those who endure it, while those who despise their days of adversity will never know the joy of it. No believer has ever regretted the silence of meekness and humility, no matter what the cost. No woman has ever wished to leave words of mercy and reconciliation unsaid, even at the cost of perishing while expressing them. No man has ever looked back with sorrow on the brief pleasures of this life or temporal gain that he has sacrificed for the name of Christ. Rewards for faithfulness often follow acts of fidelity, but the joy of the hard way comes only to those who endure the cross of Jesus Christ.

Jesus said that we are and will be persecuted in the same way as the enemy "persecuted the prophets who were before you" (Matt. 5:12), because they stood for God no matter what the consequences. He was underscoring the fact that there is comfort in the hard way that results from knowing that when you are persecuted, you belong to a long and great succession of those who have suffered this noble tradition. It is the kind of assurance that lies dormant in every righteous heart, but leaps to action under fire to help us remain strong and confident during a crisis.

The apostle Paul demonstrated how we should handle life in the hard way and thus experience the joy promised by Jesus. On his missionary trip to Lystra (with Barnabas, whose name means "son of exhortation and consolation") the "Jews came from Antioch and Iconium, and having won over the crowds, they stoned Paul and dragged him out of the city, supposing him to be dead" (Acts 14:19). Well, I would have expected that when Paul recovered consciousness he would have packed up, shook the dust off his feet, cursed those cruel persecutors, and quickly moved on to the next town to preach the gospel before his opponents appeared again. But not so. This student of the hard way did not run or hide, or complain or gripe about his situation. "But while the disciples stood around him, he got up and entered the city" (verse 20) and preached as though nothing had happened before. The people were so astonished by his resilience and commitment to the cause of Christ that many believed and became followers of the Leader of the hard way. The next day Paul and Barnabas left for Derbe. Sometime shortly thereafter "they returned to Lystra and to Iconium and to Antioch, *strengthening the souls of the disciples, encouraging them to continue in the faith, and saying, 'Through many tribulations we must enter the kingdom of God'* " (Acts 14:21, 22).

Sometimes I find it difficult to believe that these were regular human beings like me. I know that oftentimes when I hear simple criticism about me—even if it is justified—I don't want to go back to the same place and minister. Instead, I want to run and hide in shame and embarrassment. Once I remember wearing a wig on a subway train. It got caught in the door as it closed and was yanked off my head as the train pulled out jerkily from the station. Even though the car I occupied was packed with strangers, I was so filled with shame and embarrassment that it took several months before I could ride that train and use that station. Paul was physically beaten. Perhaps his clothes were torn off him, exposing him in many embarrassing ways before the people he was attempting to persuade. But although left for dead, he returned to that very place to preach in spite of the potential danger of further persecution.

"Behold, an hour is coming," Jesus said, "and has already come, for you to be scattered, each to his own home, and to leave Me alone; and yet I am not alone, because the Father is with Me. These things I have spoken to you, so that in Me you may have peace. *In the world you have tribulation, but take courage; I have overcome the world"* (John 16:32, 33).

"Indeed, all who desire to live godly in Christ Jesus will be persecuted" (2 Tim. 3:12; see also John 15:20; 1 John 3:13; Rev. 12:7-17).

Moses was persecuted, Samuel was rejected, Elijah was despised, the minor prophet Micah was hated, Nehemiah was oppressed and defamed, Jeremiah met with violent opposition from princes, priests, and his own people, and Daniel got thrown into a lions' den. In the New Testament a mob stoned Stephen to death; Herod martyred James, the brother of John; Peter and John were placed in prison; and Paul experienced long periods of persecution.

Jesus Christ, "the author and perfecter of faith" (Heb. 12:2), was persecuted more than anyone who has ever lived. The greatest of the prophets, the grandest apostle, the most illustrious martyr, He behaved magnanimously toward His tormentors, leaving believers a rich legacy of how to face the terror of tribulation and persecution.

Christian suffering has something vicarious in it. "For to you it has been granted for Christ's sake, not only to believe in Him, but also to suffer for His sake" (Phil. 1:29; see also Col. 1:24). Jesus must be so dear to us that we are ready and willing to suffer to the utmost for Him. Consequently, Christians are not to revile, slander, insult, or verbally abuse their persecutors. As a matter of fact, our witness may so move some of our persecutors that they may later join the faith of Jesus Christ.

"When we are reviled, we bless; when we are persecuted, we endure; when we are slandered, we try to conciliate; we have become as the scum of the world, the dregs of all things, even until now" (1 Cor. 4:12, 13).

Paul said he did "not write these things to shame [us], but to admonish [us] as . . . beloved children" (verse 14), so that we would not be tempted to treat our persecutors in the same way they punish us. We are not to repay evil with evil.

I can testify to this truth. During my hedonistic years as an executive assistant to the mayor of Hartford, Connecticut, I used to try to humiliate Christians publicly by calling them "Jesus freaks." Once I remember receiving an invitation to dinner at the home of a friend who had recently been "saved." He had prepared a delicious-looking salad from his garden. When we sat down to eat, he began to pray. Incensed, I pushed my chair from the table, blurted out a litany of expletives, and threatened to leave if he did not stop at once. He kept his eyes closed and continued to pray as if there had been no interruption. I stormed out of his house to the sound of his words asking God to save me. I never saw or spoke to him again. Years later, after my own conversion, I tried to contact him to let him know that his prayer had been answered, but he had moved, and I could not locate him. What a surprise it will be for him when we meet again in heaven.

I believe it was John Newton who said that the greatest surprise in heaven will be that some we expected to be there will not be, that others we did not anticipate making it will, and most of all, that we ourselves are there.

Christians are to consider sufferings and persecutions as blessings, because we have the opportunity to share the experience of Jesus Christ.

Paul said: "For I consider that the sufferings of this present time are not worthy to be compared with the glory that is to be revealed to us" (Rom. 8:18). Persecution—through the Holy Spirit—will make a believer mature in Christ. So when it comes, let us not run, hide, or complain about it, but rejoice.

But just because this may be the case, Christians should not court persecution, for there is a time and place for everything. Listen to the caution given by the One who also promised that the persecuted would be happy. "But whenever they persecute you in one city, flee to the next" (Matt. 10:23). The idea here is that we must, under the guidance of the Holy Spirit, be discerning enough to know when to flee and when to face persecution.

Jesus Himself rarely did anything to protect Himself when severely persecuted by the religious leaders. Yet, on one occasion, after a scathing encounter with the scribes and Pharisees who were angry with Him and sought to kill Him because His disciples violated their traditions and He refused to reprimand them (Matt. 15:1-9), Jesus "withdrew into the district of Tyre and Sidon" (verse 21). He fled to safety among pagans while His irate opponents cooled off in Jerusalem.

Rejoice and be exceedingly glad when you encounter persecution, for yours is the kingdom of heaven. It is the same reward promised to the poor in spirit at the beginning of the Beatitudes to ensure believers that they are the children of the kingdom of heaven. The joy of the hard way is experienced best in the fact that it leads the believer to God's kingdom. The ones who possess the kingdom did not come to do so because they persevered through persecution; they endured because they possessed the kingdom. It's in their heart, mind, soul, and body, where no persecutor's weapon can encroach or destroy.

This heavenly treasure cannot be earned—it is a gift from God—but there is a special joy, or happiness, for those who remain faithful despite the pressure on them. No one knows the world's demonic power until they reject it to accept and embrace the kingdom of God. Then the arrogant and clamorous world powers and principalities gather against them to persecute and drive them to despair.

The world has countless ways of persecuting Christ's followers. The fact that the Lord dwells in them provokes the hostility of the wicked. It is Christ in the persecuted believer that Satan seeks to destroy. Thus believers experience persecution for His sake.

During the Boxer Rebellion in China the insurgents captured a mission station and blocked all the gates but one, placing a cross flat on the ground before it. They then passed the word to those inside that any who trampled the cross underfoot would be permitted their freedom, but any who refused would be shot to death.

Terribly frightened, the first seven students ran over the cross, trampling it under their feet. The rebels let them go as promised, but the eighth student, a young girl, refused to commit such a sacrilegious act. Instead, she knelt before the cross and prayed for strength, then stood up, stepped carefully around the cross, and went out to face the firing squad. Strengthened and inspired by her example, every one of the remaining 92 students followed her to death. They discovered what many martyrs before them had—that persecutors may take the life we cannot keep, but cannot harm the life we receive from Jesus and cannot lose.

CHAPTER

10

The Search for Significance

"Happy are ye whenever [people] may reproach you, and may persecute, and may say any evil thing against you falsely for my sake—rejoice ye and be glad, because your reward [is] great in the heavens, for thus did they persecute the prophets who were before you." Matthew 5:11, 12, YLT.

Ever since his exile from heaven Satan has worked tirelessly to destroy God's people (Rev. 12:7-17). He has used every possible means to misrepresent God and mislead His children. False accusation is one of his strongest weapons against us.

The tragic results of an incident in a small town of North Dakota bear this out. It happened to a Christian family who were relatively happy, even though the mother had been suffering from severe postpartum depression since the recent birth of her second child. She and her husband clung to their faith in Jesus Christ, who blessed them with the ability to continue enjoying their home and family despite the wife's battle with depression. The neighbors observed the warmth in their relationship and marveled at their living faith, especially in view of her struggles with the emotional pain. In spite of the negative thoughts that haunted her every day, she was able, with the guidance of a dedicated physician and her commitment to Christ, to function almost normally, even to the point of greeting her husband every evening at the gate with their two small children.

Sometimes there were a few tears, but laughter and prayer still reigned in their home. When the weather was good, father and children would romp together on the back lawn while the mother watched from the window. Then one day a village gossip started a story that the father was being unfaithful to his wife. It had absolutely no foundation, but when it eventually came to the ears of the young wife, it had devastating results.

Even though intellectually she knew that it could not be true, and no matter how many times she remembered his generosity toward the family and tenderness toward her, she was too emotionally fragile to keep her mind focused on the real facts. The fabricated details of her husband's supposed infidelity were more than she could bear.

One evening when her husband came home no one met him at the gate, no fragrant aroma came from the kitchen. His heart chilled with fear as he unlocked the door of his home that fateful day.

All day long he had had a disturbing premonition that something had gone terribly wrong. Fearing the worst—that the postpartum depression had finally overwhelmed his wife—he quickly searched his home, praying all the time that she had simply gone for a stroll with the children and would be back any moment. But when he ran down the steps into the basement, his worst fears were confirmed. He found the three members of his family hanging from a beam in the darkened room that they had recently remodeled.

The young mother had apparently never heard the Japanese proverb that urges one to believe only half of what is heard after thoroughly checking the source of the rumor. Overwhelmed by the deep depression that she fought every day, she took the lives of her two children, then her own. In the days that followed the funerals, the truth of what had happened came out. Satan had used a gossip's tongue to destroy a family.

The vast majority of us will never murder our children or commit suicide, but all of us struggle with the presence and pain of false accusations. Nobody but the victim and perpetrator knows the troubles that the righteous experience for Christ's name and sake. Some are of Goliath proportions. Others—the ones that linger longest, are hardest to eliminate, and do the most damage—are the little thorns that choke the Word out of our hearts so that we eventually become unfruitful (Mark 4:7, 19).

When an opponent—especially a relative, a friend, or a member of the body of believers—approaches us with the statement "*If* you are a Christian," it is like a knife being twisted in the heart. We want to fight back, to vindicate our character. But we should call upon every resource in our divinely provided arsenal to resist the temptation, especially since the Bible cautions us against such behavior.

"The Lord's bond-servant must not be quarrelsome, but be kind to all, able to teach, patient when wronged, with gentleness correcting those who are in opposition, if perhaps God may grant them repentance leading to the knowledge of the truth" (2 Tim. 2:24, 25).

As others attack us it is easy to forget that the Bible urges us to "never pay back evil for evil to anyone" (Rom. 12:17). On the other hand, society expects us to fight for our rights. We justify our failure to obey the divine command by protesting that everyone is standing up for theirs. The Inspired Word teaches that we should not be "bold to class or compare ourselves with some of those who commend themselves; [for] when they measure themselves by themselves and compare themselves with themselves, they are without understanding" (2 Cor. 10:12).

Ultimately, to ignore this warning is to succumb to the temptation to define our personal worth by how others esteem our possessions, attainments, successes, or failures. We need to learn—and practice—the biblical exhortation that we are Abba's beloved children and that only our loving Father is worthy—or able—to judge or commend us adequately.

Today's generation suffers especially from verbal abuse, particularly victims of domestic violence. We have allowed television to convince us that insulting others is a sign of affection and an acceptable mode of communication. "Celebrity roasts" have people lining up to say all manner of insulting and shameful things about the one being "honored" at expensive dinners and political fund-raisers. Such "honorees" include even former and present national presidents who gladly embrace being roasted. They add self-deprecating stories to those of their guests to show they are good sports—and to boost their public opinion ratings!

Where "roasting" is popular among the rich, to "dis" (slang for "disrespect, be contemptuous about, or insult") someone has been a form of verbal abuse common on the "streets." It is an unbelievably raw way of talking down to and about others, using the most obscene terms. Whereas participants in a roast may avoid insulting mothers and verbally abusing those with disabilities, dissing respects no one. Unfortunately, over the past few decades this offensive type of speech has wormed its way into the language of mainstream America through popular television programs, movies, and rap songs.

Verbal abuse is no longer the domain of the street and entertainment industry. It has also become popular among some preachers, who use their pulpits as a way of verbally beating up their congregations week after week. What is quite amazing is that people, in their desperate search for meaning in life, pack the halls of such preachers and give millions of dollars in offerings. It almost seems that the worse they get treated, the more they contribute to the demands of what appears to be an extension of domestic violence in the spiritual community.

Not only must we face these major forms of abuse; we also have to deal with countless little thorns that fester and drain away our spiritual, emotional, moral, and often physical energies.

How then must we deal with the ninth beatitude, which says, Happy "are you when people insult you, persecute you, and falsely say all kinds of evil against you" (NIV) because of Jesus?

It is as if God is saying: "Listen to me, you that know what is right, who have my teaching fixed in your hearts. Do not be afraid when people taunt and insult you; [one day] they will vanish like moth-eaten clothing! But the deliverance I bring will last forever; my victory will endure for all time" (Isa. 51:7, 8, TEV).

Now that we are fortified for this last leg of our journey through this section of the Sermon on the Mount, let us notice that when Jesus delivered His final beatitude He made a deliberate change of focus as He addressed His disciples. Up until that time it seemed as though He had not singled them out as He preached His sermon. Now, however, He spoke directly to the disciples as He urged them to "walk in a manner worthy of the calling with which [they had] been called" (Eph. 4:1). From a study of the Greek text and its different shades of meaning, the reader gets the strong impression that Jesus looked them square in the eyes, perhaps even pointed at them for emphasis, and said, "Happy are *you,"* My disciples and immediate followers.

Jesus was underscoring their personal involvement and experience by saying, "You who have given up everything to accept and accompany Me, who are about to learn how to excel in the virtues emphasized in previous beatitudes, must reckon upon more difficulties, hardships, and trials than others. But don't be afraid, or let your hearts be troubled, or allow disappointment and despair to rob you of your precious reward" (see John 14:1, 2). Instead, "rejoice and be glad, for your reward in heaven is great" (Matt. 5:12).

To further encourage the disciples not to faint under affront of any kind, but to realize that they were part of a succession of giants of faith whose actions glorified God, Jesus pointed to the ancient prophets who had endured persecution. It took some 30 years, after many of his colleagues had been martyred and some had renounced their faith in Jesus, for Peter to understand by experience what He said. When Peter did, he was able to strengthen and encourage the fledgling Christian church. He wrote:

"Beloved, do not be surprised at the fiery ordeal among you, which comes upon you for your testing, as though some strange thing were happening to you; but to the degree that you share the sufferings of Christ, keep on rejoicing, so that also at the revelation of His glory you may rejoice with exultation. If you are reviled for the name of Christ, you are blessed [happy], because the Spirit of glory and of God rests on you. Make sure that none of you suffers as a murderer, or thief, or evildoer, or a troublesome meddler; but if anyone suffers as a Christian, he is not to be ashamed, but is to glorify God in this name" (1 Peter 4:12-16).

Jesus did not say, "Happy are you *if* people insult, persecute, or falsely say all kinds of evil things against you." He used *when* to underscore the certainty of such experiences as He forewarned His followers so that they would be adequately forearmed against such trials. Before we move on, it is important that we understand the original meaning of these words that depict those trials and tribulations. Modern English versions of the Bible sanitize some of the terms.

The ancient world of Jesus considered words much more powerful than society does today. Almost every word evoked strong images or feelings. For example, the word "name" in today's English describes the distinctive designation, title, or identification of a person or thing. Back then, it meant these things, but most important, a "name" conveyed the character of its bearer.

We are urged to pray "in the name of Jesus" and ask "anything in His name" (see John 14:13, 14). It does not mean that we must end our prayers by saying "in the name of Jesus." Rather, it is an appeal for believers to imitate our Lord's life and practice His teachings so that when we ask in His name, we are literally presenting ourselves before God in His character.

Let us now examine the word "insult" from this final beatitude. Jesus could have chosen any one of several words in the *Koine* (the everyday

Greek language of the New Testament). He selected a word that also means "to reproach, upbraid, revile, or verbally abuse." In addition to the expressions of rebuke and disapproval people used against Jesus, they labeled Him with derogatory nicknames that people later used against His followers (Matt. 10:24-28).

For example, the religious leaders called Him a Samaritan who had a demon (John 8:48). They accused Him of being demon-possessed and insane (John 10:20), and taunted Him about the questionable circumstances of His birth, implying that He had been born of "fornication" (John 8:41). Those seeking to kill Him impugned His integrity (John 7:25). And as He hung helplessly on the cross they insulted Him (Matt. 27:39-44). Yet "while being reviled, He did not revile in return; while suffering, He uttered no threats, but kept entrusting Himself to Him who judges righteously" (1 Peter 2:23).

As terrible as it must have been for the disciples to hear, especially at the very beginning of their ministry, Jesus emphasized the reproach and contemptuous names they would endure. He knew that if they were properly informed of events before they occurred, His disciples—both then and now—would be strengthened when they experienced the fulfillment of His words.

While it is true that silence is golden in most situations of persecution (Matt. 26:63; 27:12, 14) and that Christians should bless others even when reviled (1 Cor. 4:12) and not attempt to justify themselves in the fires of adversity, we do not always have to flee from our enemies or refuse to respond. Nor do we always have to give in and buckle under their cruel attacks. When we come under fire, we can stand firm and be aware that there will come a time when our opponents will have to give account before God for their actions (Jude 15).

We can also exercise our God-given and legitimate rights and rebuke our accusers, as Jesus did on some occasions (Mark 14:62). Although no one wants to face the world's contempt, Jesus has called us to follow in His footsteps, to imitate His example as we suffer for His sake (Phil. 1:29).

When Jesus began the Beatitudes, He promised that those who possess nothing can still be happy. He ended these principles by establishing that those who are reviled or insulted (and note that for the first time He makes it personal) because of Him or His name, i.e., character, will also be happy.

In order to attain this happiness, we must put aside self-defense, self-vindication, and self-justification, and make no attempt to excuse "self" either in our own eyes or before God. We must understand that in the kingdom of grace those who insist on defending themselves will have their own "selves" as their defense and nothing else—not even the divine Advocate. But those who come defenseless before God and their persecutors will have God Himself as their defender.

Scripture also assures us that those who have gone the way of Cain and Balaam and "revile the things which they do not understand; and the things which they know by instinct, like unreasoning animals, by these things they are destroyed" (Jude 10). Furthermore, if we truly believe that we bring nothing to our salvation and live only by His grace, then when others attack and reproach us for Jesus, we should not try to justify ourselves.

Remember that the meek person does not care what the world thinks of them. They long ago decided that the world's esteem is not worth the effort it demands. Why, then, do we bristle and complain when the world ignores or rejects us, especially since we are quick to say that we are "nothing in God's sight" and call ourselves a worm or dust? Where is our consistency? Come on, we are made of stronger stock than that! We are not going to let that old world, or the devil, turn us around, are we?

A. W. Tozer said: "Think for yourself whether much of your sorrow has not risen from someone speaking slightingly of you. As long as you set yourself up as a little god to which you must be loyal there will be those who will delight to offer affront to your idol. . . . The heart's fierce effort to protect itself from every slight, to shield its touchy honor from the bad opinion of friend and enemy, will never let the mind have rest. Continue this fight through the years and the burden will become intolerable" (*The Pursuit of God,* p. 106).

It is true that in ourselves we are nothing, but in and to God we are everything. As a matter of fact, if we really accept this, then when we are insulted and verbally abused we won't take it so personally. Why? Because we "have been crucified with Christ; and it is no longer [we] who live, but Christ lives in [us]; and the life which [we] now live in the flesh [we] live by faith in the Son of God, who loved [us] and gave Himself up for [us]" (Gal. 2:20).

Most of the false accusations that believers will face come from those who profess faith in God, not from nonbelievers (Matt. 26:59). In order to accomplish their evil goals, God's modern-day religious opponents defame and misrepresent His true followers. They cannot look His children in the face because the light that shines from their faces would cause them to flee from their presence as if before God Himself. Yet they really think that they are doing the Lord's service by attacking others. They do not realize that it is not God's work to drive others out of His loving arms with harsh criticism or human opinions, rules, and doctrines.

On the other hand, true Christians will do nothing harsh and unkind to court their insults. We should avoid discussions that offend others or undermine the understanding and denominational choices of other believers even as we attempt to point them to the real truth in Jesus Christ.

"The Lord's bond-servant must not be quarrelsome, but be kind to all, able to teach, patient when wronged, with gentleness correcting those who are in opposition, if perhaps God may grant them repentance leading to the knowledge of the truth" (2 Tim. 2:24, 25).

When God's people experience persecution, they must also remember the tremendous power they have from their heavenly Father and patiently show that they can bear up as their Elder Brother, Jesus, did (1 Peter 3:13-18). If and when we do suffer persecution, then, in our faithful endeavors to be Christlike, we should remember the ancient prophets and thousands of believers before us who have been mistreated, even to the point of death.

We are to focus on the fact that it is really Christ and His righteousness in us that others are maligning (Ps. 69:9; Rom. 8:36). That is the reason Jesus emphasized "because of *Me*" in this beatitude. When He stopped Saul on his way to Damascus, the risen Savior asked, "Why are you persecuting *Me?*" (Acts 9:4).

The blood of martyrs is said to be the seed of the Christian church, so much so that generation after generation regarded persecution as a great privilege. Somehow our generation has lost that concept. Groaning and complaining at the slightest disturbance in our experience, instead of confidently enduring, we quickly blame God for not rescuing or delivering us. We need to be exceedingly glad as we learn to practice perseverance, coming to the place where we can accept suffering as a great privilege and not something to mourn (Rom. 8:17, 18). While we should not solicit persecution, when it does come we ought to embrace it as one of the chief blessings in the believer's life.

Jesus used two strong expressions—"rejoice" and be "exceedingly glad" (NKJV)—that also connote the joy of the saints over the marriage of the Lamb (Rev. 19:7). The first word, "rejoice" *(chairete),* comes from the root *(charis)* for "grace," which describes occasions of pleasure, delight, and causes of favorable regard that are gifts from God. The emphasis is on the energy, freedom, and universality of expression it brings into the life of His suffering children. Its spontaneous character, in the face of adversity and persecution, results from God's redemptive mercy and the pleasures He designs for those who endure to the end.

The word for "exceedingly glad," *agalliasthe,* scholars generally translate as "rejoice" (see Luke 10:21), but it should be rendered "exceedingly glad by leaping for joy." It describes the response of someone who is rescued from disaster or is victorious in an impossible mission. According to tradition, its Hebrew counterpart, *gil,* describes the dance Abraham is reported to have done after God entered into a solemn covenant with him (see Gen. 15). Jesus Himself affirmed that Abraham performed this dance (John 8:56). From the time of Jesus until now, it has been a Jewish tradition for the bridegroom to perform such a dance, as we see demonstrated in the popular play *Fiddler on the Roof.*

King David leaped and danced with abandon before the Lord as he joyfully led the procession bearing the ark to Jerusalem (2 Sam. 6:16). His wife, Michal, displeased with his exuberance, criticized him (verse 20). So deep was her anger over his expressions of happiness that, after his public display and unusual worship activities, she rejected him and was never intimate with him again. As a result, she "had no child to the day of her death" (verse 23). The worshiping community of God is always home to two groups: the Davids who thank Him for deliverance with leaping and dancing, and the Michals who honor dignity more than Deity.

When the disciples returned from their mission journey, Jesus also danced the *gil.* He leaped with exceeding joy in the rhythm and choreography of the true Bridegroom (see Luke 10:17-21, in which English versions generally translate the word *agalliasato* as "rejoiced" in verse 21).

Paul and Silas seemed to have been exceedingly glad as they unabashedly praised God in their jail cell (Acts 16:25). Their actions not only attracted the attention of their jailer, but also brought about his conversion and that of his entire household (verses 31-40).

John the revelator enjoined believers at the second coming of Christ to respond in gratitude for the great grace that brought them through this world into the next. He wrote, under the inspiration of the Holy Spirit, "Let us *rejoice and be glad [agalliomen]* and give the glory to Him, for the marriage of the Lamb has come and His bride has made herself ready" (Rev. 19:7).

Watch anyone rescued from a burning building, a sinking ship, or an airplane crash. How do they react afterward? They express their relief and gratitude in uninhibited acts of happiness. Has not the Lord delivered you at least once from loneliness or death? Has He not miraculously provided money, shelter, and hope for you in situations that seemed impossible and hopeless? Did He not sacrifice His pure and sinless life so that we could be saved?

If your answer to such questions is a resounding "Yes!" then let us leap and dance as David did *before the Lord*. Let us shout and praise the Lord with sacrifices of our hearts.

> "Praise the Lord!
> Praise God in His sanctuary;
> Praise Him in His mighty expanse.
> Praise Him for His mighty deeds;
> Praise Him according to His excellent greatness.
> Praise Him with trumpet sound;
> Praise Him with harp and lyre.
> Praise Him with timbrel and dancing;
> Praise Him with stringed instruments and pipe.
> Praise Him with loud cymbals;
> Praise Him with resounding cymbals.
> Let everything that has breath praise the Lord.
> Praise the Lord!"
>
> —Psalm 150

Jesus emphasized that great rewards await those who endure persecution and are exceedingly glad during and after their ordeal. As a result of this promise, the early martyrs viewed persecution as the highest reward they could achieve. Believing the crown of persecution to be the brightest that any of the redeemed could wear, many early Christians literally sought to be martyrs by throwing themselves at their persecutors. I am not recommending a revival of that conduct, but am emphasizing that they rejoiced, sang songs, prayed, and praised God so fervently that sometimes it converted their oppressors. While many of the spectators shuddered and covered their eyes or turned their faces away with horror at the sight of the cruelties Christians suffered, the martyrs leaped for joy at the prospect of death for the sake of Jesus.

The authorities forced some Christians to walk over sharpened nails or sharpened shells. Others, after suffering the most excruciating tortures devised by their persecutors, were scourged until their skin peeled off their body. But they sang, prayed, and praised the Lord with such astonishing courage that many unbelievers became converts to a faith that could inspire such fortitude and bravery.

Almost every Christian has heard the story of Polycarp, the bishop of Smyrna, who, when arrested for his faith in Jesus Christ, gave a great feast for the guards who apprehended him. He asked their permission to pray, and after he did so for an hour in their hearing, they repented that they would be instrumental in his death.

But they still escorted him before the proconsul, who urged Polycarp to renounce Christ, saying, "Swear, and I will release thee—reproach Christ!" The aged bishop stood his ground, replying, "Eighty and six years I have served Him, and He never once wronged me. How then shall I blaspheme my King, who has saved me?"

The proconsul angrily condemned the old man to be burned to death in the marketplace. When the guards tied Polycarp to the stake, not nailed, as was the custom, he sang, prayed, praised God, and stood immovable as the flames encircled his body. To the surprise of his persecutors and the spectators, the flames did not touch him, so the proconsul ordered him pierced with a sword, but the blood gushed out of his wound with such force that it extinguished the fire. Finally, the enemies of the gospel ordered the guards to build a bigger bonfire that eventually consumed Polycarp. He could be heard singing loudly until the last breath left his body.

Although God does not desire or require that we seek persecution, He does provide an incentive for those who do suffer tribulation. He promises a reward in heaven and comfort while on earth:

First, they are happy, because they receive hardship in this lifetime

(Luke 16:25). Woe to those who receive theirs after the final resurrection (Rev. 20:15). Happy because it is an honor to suffer for Christ's name and sake (Acts 5:41), they regard such affliction as nothing when compared to the promised glory (Rom. 8:18), and embrace it as an opportunity to experience vicariously some of the sufferings of Jesus as well as to receive generous outpourings of grace (verses 28, 29).

Second, they will be recompensed on earth. Scripture calls those who exult in their trials and tribulations (Rom. 5:3) the salt of the earth (Matt. 5:13) and recognizes them as the light of the world (verse 14). They will also receive rewards in heaven, where God will dwell among them (Rev. 21:1-3) and they shall be His people (1 Peter 2:9).

Notice that their reward awaits them in heaven and not on earth. There it is safe from chance, fraud, or violence. Believers who remain faithful to Christ have not only a sure title to the kingdom of heaven (according to previous promises in some of these beatitudes), but a crown awaiting them in heaven. Paul said: "In the future there is laid up for me the crown of righteousness, which the Lord, the righteous Judge, will award to me on that day; and not only to me, but to all who have loved His appearing" (2 Tim. 4:8).

Third, Scripture ranks them among the great men and women of faith throughout human history, for Jesus said we would be treated in the same way as the persecuted prophets who came before us.

Wicked people mocked the prophet Isaiah, then, according to legend, stuffed him into the hollowed-out trunk of a tree and sawed him in two (Heb. 11:37). Jezebel threatened Elijah's life after he stood up against hordes of her pagan prophets on Mount Carmel (1 Kings 19:2).

God's true prophets were maligned, beaten, and sometimes put to death. Therefore, we should not regard persecution as something strange. We must not murmur about our adversities because God does not prevent them or speedily deliver us. Instead, we must see in the stories of the prophets that God's grace was sufficient for them and will sustain us now. Having been justified by faith, we have peace with God and must consider it an honor to be included among such great leaders of faith.

Finally, our search for substance ends in Jesus Christ, Lord and Master of our lives forever and ever. You might feel as if you are already being persecuted right now. Someone, for example, may have accused you falsely, and the pain of that betrayal is almost too much to bear. No matter how much you love Jesus, confess faith in Him, or worship and praise Him, still the anguish lingers on. You go from seminar to seminar, listen to the sermons of the best speakers of our day, read every new book on grace and prayer, all the while hoping that something will be said or done to eliminate the pain and suffering. But the rhythm of pain is relentless.

Some of us keep hoping that God will use us in a big or mighty way so that we will find purpose in life. When He doesn't heal and help us in the time and way that we plead, the disappointment can be searing. Then, almost too late, we discover that it is only in Jesus Christ that we find the happiness that ends the search for the one thing we were made for and desperately need—unconditional love and regard. He wants us to absorb this gift, to own it, to let it pervade our very being as does the blood in our veins and the breath in our nostrils. Then we will be happy believers even in the face of the severest persecution.

Many never attain this promised happiness, because they neglect to seek it in the way pointed out by Jesus in His sermon on the mount. The principles in the Beatitudes will assuredly lead to everlasting happiness. Such blessedness is ours for the taking. There's no need to be timid. We're not trespassing on forbidden ground, nor do we have to sneak in under the cover of darkness and greedily grasp as much as our arms can hold before we get caught and punished.

Through the Beatitudes God has actually invited us to come into the kingdom and enjoy its resources. He tells us that we may confidently approach His throne, where we will receive mercy for our failures and find all the help we need (Heb. 4:16). The Lord calls us to come rejoicing, exceedingly glad and leaping for joy, to the marriage of the Lamb. "[Happy *(makarioi)*] are those who are invited to the marriage supper of the Lamb" (Rev. 19:9).

Accept it and don't be late for this celebration of all celebrations. It begins today. "Believe Me," Jesus said, "this will make you very happy!"

Epilogue

"Happiness isn't based on what you do for God. It is based on who you are in Him. Happiness is truly being a child of our Father in heaven."—Dallas Holm.

An American diplomat who was also a renown storyteller finally met his match in a most unlikely manner. On a visit to central Africa he tried to impress the nationals with his great talent by relating a lengthy anecdote. When he finished, his interpreter turned to his country-men and said only four words. To the diplomat's surprise, everyone burst out laughing, accompanied by thunderous applause.

"How could you tell the story so quickly and receive such a reaction?" the wide-eyed diplomat exclaimed.

"Story too long," the interpreter replied, "so I say, 'He tell joke. Laugh!' "

Many in the medical profession recognize laughter as one of the greatest mental tonics known to humanity. Studies on peace of mind and happiness, conducted by some of the most reputable scientists and prestigious universities, have discovered that laughter improves our health in many ways not yet fully explored or understood. Considered, next to love, to be the second most powerful human emotion, laughter is said to be able to dispel anxiety and help control depression, fear, and worry. Laughter provides physical, psychological, social, and even spir-itual benefits. It enhances the respiratory system, helps oxygenate the body, relaxes tense nerves and muscles, and is an all-around painkiller. Besides lowering your pulse rate and blood pressure, laughter can pave the way for a new outlook on life. The universal communicator that crosses all boundaries of race, culture, class, and religion, it is the sure sign of happiness.

Why, then, did Jesus not recommend this simplest, cheapest, and most enjoyable gift instead of just the word "happy" in the Beatitudes? Perhaps because just as the Ten Commandments demonstrate God's character, so the Beatitudes describe the person and personality of Jesus, which He wants every believer to have and develop in their relationship with Him.

For example, Jesus was "poor in spirit." The descriptions of His humble beginnings (Luke 2:1-20) and His adult years as an itinerant preacher (Matt. 8:20) are but a few of the reports of the material poverty He endured on earth so that we could inherit the riches of heaven. Jesus was also intimately acquainted with grief. He mourned both publicly and privately (Matt. 14:13; John 11:35; and Matt. 26:36-46), but unlike His gift of comfort to us, He found Himself abandoned and betrayed by His closest friends and associates. Yet, from all reports, He was a happy human whose presence even children sought.

Jesus was also meek. In fact, one of the few instances of His giving a self-portrait includes this characteristic (Matt. 11:29). He hungered and thirsted for righteousness. It would be an understatement to say that He was merciful, i.e., kind, to His known enemies. Scripture repeatedly confirms this characteristic, especially the healing of one who accompanied His opponents to arrest Him (Luke 22:47-51) and His appeal for the forgiveness of those who crucified Him (Luke 23:34).

When it comes to being pure in heart, no one who has ever lived on the earth was His equal (Heb. 4:15). He was the peacemaker par excellence, so much so that the Bible refers to Him as the Prince of Peace (Isa. 9:6). Not only was He a peacemaker on earth, but He made peace between sinners and God (2 Cor. 5:18).

No one, not even the greatest martyrs, ever endured the persecution for the sake of righteousness that Jesus experienced. So horrific was His ordeal from birth to death that John declared: "He came to His own, and those who were His own did not receive Him" (John 1:11). Do I need to describe the insults and false accusations He endured? (see Matt. 26:57-68).

In spite of such a hard life on earth, no one was happier than Jesus. "For consider Him who has endured such hostility by sinners against Himself so that you will not grow weary and lose heart" (Heb. 12:3).

Because of "the joy set before Him" of knowing that one day you and I would be reconciled to our heavenly Father through His life of suffering and sacrifice, He "endured the cross, despising the shame, and has sat down at the right hand of the throne of God" (verse 2).

That's what I want! Isn't that your goal in life? Do you not also desperately desire to be happy no matter what the circumstance or situation? Do you seek to be seated (in close proximity and intimate relationship) at the right hand of our heavenly Father and His Christ? That's happiness to me—to be close to Christ. But to accomplish that, we must be like Jesus, whose character we find portrayed in the Beatitudes.

God wants His prodigal children to come home and occupy their places at the right hand of His throne in a committed relationship with Him. He longs for us to accept His gift of happiness right now. It really doesn't matter where you've been, what you've done, where you are, or what you're doing right now. Just come home and be reconciled to your Father in heaven. He is eagerly awaiting your return with a garland of happiness that is just right for your heart and head.

We are much like a young girl who was raised by loving Christian parents, but got drawn away by the bright attractions of the city she saw portrayed in magazines. After she left her home to study at a faraway college, she began living a life that led her into the bowels of darkness to support her sinful habits. She cut off any contact with her parents and moved several times so that they could not locate her. As the months passed into years, her father died. Her mother tried to find her, but without success.

One day, in desperation, the woman hired a private investigator to help in her search for her prodigal daughter. The investigator had the brilliant idea of making copies of the mother's photograph with two words, "Come Home," printed beneath the portrait. Then he placarded every known location where the daughter had once lived and every haunt she was reported to have frequented. He left photos at bus and train stations and missions and pasted them on lampposts and boarded-up buildings.

Not long after, the daughter was leaving one of her favorite hideaways when she stepped on a paper on the pavement. It became stuck to the heel of her shoe. When she bent down to remove it, she came face to face with the portrait of her mother. The tears ran down her cheeks so heavily that she could hardly read the two words: "Come Home."

Immediately she made the long journey to her old home, but when she arrived, she was nervous about ringing the bell and seeing her parents again. She paced and pondered, then folded her arms as she leaned against the front door. The weight of her body caused the door to give way. It instantly swung wide open, and she fell into the hall of her old home, where her mother was asleep in a rocking chair near the door.

Her mother had anxiously waited and watched, from that vantage point, since the daughter had left home. With tears in her eyes and arms wide open, the woman quickly pulled her daughter to her feet and into a warm embrace. She covered her with kisses as she said, "My dear daughter, the door has never been locked since you went away."

The door of God's great heart of love and compassion has never been closed or locked against His sinful, erring children, whom He loves above all. We ravish His heart so much so that He sacrificed His only begotten Son to bring us home. He has prepared a place in His kingdom for us that eyes have not seen and our minds cannot imagine. Mere words cannot describe its beauty, peace, and happiness. Instead, we have to experience it personally. The door is wide open now, and Jesus is calling you. He is appealing on behalf of His Father, through the still small voice of the Holy Spirit, saying, "My beloved, weary, and miserable children, *come home.*"

Just come on home, sit right down, and let the grace of God shower you with joy on earth, as it is in heaven. Don't you long for the peace, passion, and splendor God has for your personal wholeness and spiritual maturity? The thought awakens fervent devotion to Him right now, doesn't it? Come on, then, let's not keep Him waiting any longer. Let's go home—right now!

Happy are *you* who hear and answer His call! I'll see you at the banquet in heaven. We're going to have a ball with Jesus!